Varieties of Homage

Varieties of Homage

John Matthias

ODD VOLUMES

Odd Volumes
of
The Fortnightly Review

CHAVAGNES-EN-PAILLERS

2022

ODD VOLUMES

The Fortnightly Review
96 rue du Calvaire
85250 Chavagnes-en-Paillers

France.

Published for subscribers.

info@fortnightlyreview.co.uk

ISBN 978-0-9997058-1-0

Contents

INSTEAD OF A FOREWORD

PART I. DES PETITS HOMMAGES

PART II. HOMAGE TO C. P. CAVAFY

PART III. HOMAGE TO PETER TAYLOR
BY WAY OF GEORGE GARRETT

PART IV. HOMAGE TO HACHESTON
HALT AND OTHER STOPS

PART V. HOMAGES TO SOME
MASTERS AND SOME FRIENDS

PART VI. DES PETITS HOMMAGES

PART VII. CÉLESTE, MARCEL, VINTEUIL, AND JUSTICE

INSTEAD OF AN EPILOGUE

Instead of a Foreword

Both English and French poetry have a long tradition of Homages, or *Hommages*. I especially like the use of the French plural masculine noun, *presenter ses hommages*: to pay one's respects. I try to do that in this book, try to pay my respects to poems, poets, friends, traditions, and places.

*

One of the principal functions of poetry. . . . is the preservation and renewal of natural piety toward every kind of created excellence, toward the great creatures like the sun, moon, and earth on which our lives depend, toward the brave warrior, the wise man, the beautiful woman.

W. H. Auden, "The Dyer's Hand"

*

Homage / Elegy / Translation / *Hommages*

*

The Alexandria to which Cavafy returned had gone through a series of distressing upheavals of which the British bombardment in 1882 had been only the beginning. Egypt was now practically a dependency of England. The commercial life of the Greek community had been destroyed, and Alexandrian Greeks found it difficult to rebuild their life and their institutions in a time of general misery and decadence.

Rae Dalven, trans., *The Complete Poems of Cavafy*

*

Lives that obey you move like music,
    Becoming now what they only can be once,
Making of silence decisive sound: it sounds
    Easy, but one must find the time. Clio,

Muse of Time, but for whose merciful silence
    Only the first step would count and that
Would always be murder, whose kindness never
    Is taken in, forgive our noises

And teach us our recollections . . .

W. H. Auden, "Homage to Clio"

I

DES PETITS HOMMAGES

BEI DAO

Landscape

0

"Landscape Over Zero"

Ten men

Squared

\#

root to route over

Mandrake

mandrake

TOMAS TRANSTRÖMER

A friend had asked: *Do you hear*
the tuba blast?

O

He did, all along the coast
Or was it only in his head, drowning out the Mozart
welcoming the dead

&

Hashtag, as they say,
pressing fingers on their small machines
#stockholmarchipelago // stroke stroke

#

Sapphics, said his friend,
touching with his finger TT's living lips
that could no longer speak
Too many Sapphics

DOUGLAS KINSEY

In a three-part book, "III"
Is Douglas Kinsey's favorite poem.

0

And yet it's not a poem but only a division
a positioning
Keeping some things in and keeping some things out
A number on an otherwise blank page

III

It's not a hashtag, though.
It's Douglas Kinsey's favorite poem

In that book, anyway

and maybe in a lot of other books
as well

CAROLE SNOW

Sand garden, Kyoto and "Kyoto"
    snail   frog
      &&&

Basho in English and in "English," thank you Robert Hass
old friend

stone

          stone
&
stone

Stand

sand storm there, so goggle up the eyes and
quantum jump

blind

frog

snail

STEPHEN CRANE

Mr. Berryman insisted I account for SC's heart
1959 in Salt Lake City.
All full of Mormons
Even fuller for a week of Berryman in full flight

0

"In the desert," he said, "SC ate of his heart." I didn't
know that but I said I'd read

"The Open Boat," *The Red Badge of Courage.*

Me, just 18, and Mr. B, not yet even "Henry," sitting
in a U of Utah dormitory room,

both of us cross-legged on the floor.

"I like it because it is bitter," he said.

What? "My heart."

#

"Is it good, friend?" he asked.

I didn't know.

"I like it because it is bitter," he said.

"Anything else?" I asked.

"Oh yes," he said,

"And because it is my heart"

HART CRANE

Who also ate of his heart
and walks, stately, stately, as in some strange
procession of hypothetical Royals
on a river bank,
Jane, Jane, tall as a crane, said Dame
Edith Sitwell,
so unlikely a contemporary

0

No
He couldn't walk like that, said Uncle Yvor Winters
Often couldn't walk at all
the alcohol, you know, and otherwise he walked
all Chaplinesque
with "meek adjustments"

\#
Not the way that Father Whitman walked
if you'll admit paternity
No serenity at all for this poor man but
siren siren
Une Saison en Enfer

GUSTAF SOBIN

"I often came to know whole patches of ground in which I could expect to find, say, traces of an outdoor Neolithic atelier (scrapers, blades, burins). Other spots secreted hunting tools (lance heads, javelin points), still others yielded bounty of square-shaped, Galo-Roman bath tiles—

tesserae

ah

and trifles, truffles too

&

flies dance above the hidden things and
in the end you might
sacrifice your very being for the sacred source of
dreams that nurtured
life
up from its early grave
On an antique table notes on the finer points
of Provençal linguistics
lance heads, burins, bath tiles
a plate of truffles
love
oh slowly slowly rising from the dead for
Julieta, wife
and for her husband Cabassac

RENÉ CHAR

As if encrypted as a code by the Maquis
"Julieta" "Cabassac"
were hiding in the truffles

just as René Char was hiding in the peasant cottage
in Provençe with potent radios
understood much later by a Yank to be what powered
Paradise Lost

radi / os

"a false proximity," thought Heidegger, but just the thing
to bring the news: *télégraphie sans fils*

\#

A friend finds *notness* in all *sonnets*
while my student some years back, Yanbing Chen,
knocked at my window in the night

Saying: "Done it! Done it!"
(for a translation seminar at Notre Dame,
the university
and not the great cathedral)

& pasted his new page against the glass:
Landscape Over Zero, it said
and Yanbing said

"Surprise! I've written it in Sapphics!"

II

HOMAGE TO
C. P. CAVAFY

THE CITY

The most famous of his poems was hidden in
A drawer for fifteen years. Worked and reworked.
Aabbccdda in the first stanza; eeffggdde in the next.
We can't do that very well in English; a kind of
Eighteen-line sonnet trying to strangle itself in
Repeating sounds. He liked the rhymes, but admitted
The constraint. He wanted a powerful image of ennui,
Of deséperance. Without rhymes, I'm half done.

But with rhymes he was not. Fiddle fiddle fiddle.
Alexandria he called "a little corner of the world."
Six lines to go. He said we'd roam the same streets,
Wander among the same neighborhoods as he
Wandered and rewandered among his sixteen lines.
Now just three. He said we'd always arrive in one city
As he always arrived at his desk with the poem inside.
Take it out. Don't hope to improve it. Ruin your life.

THE GOD ABANDONS ANTONY

If the god abandoned Antony
The question is which one: Bacchus they all say,
And so says the music that our hero hears,
The bacchanals piping their way out of town.
No more grapes to crush between
His soldier's chest and Cleopatra's breasts,
Making wine between them as the sticky juice
Pours down their legs.
                    But that would have been
A good and not a bad thing for the alliance;
No more Bacchus; no more bawdy nights. Instead
Cear focus, instead decisive moves against
The enemy at the gates and sailing boldly down
The Nile. So Mars I say. It was Mars abandoned
Antony, who had the brain only of a high school
Football fumbler, halfback drunk at a loss
In a big game. *Don't leave me Bacchus*, he begs,
While Mars stares at the scene with contempt
And, wholly unnoticed, slowly walks away.

SATRAPY

He's been at his boss for a promotion
For a number of years, but CEO Artaxerxes
Finds him both a bit of a bore and a
Bit of a slacker. What he wants is to shine
In the Agora, go to concerts and plays,
Maybe even deliver a speech.

                            When Artaxerxes
Tires of the whining and begging
He finally says Okay, I'll make you a Satrap.
What's that exactly? asks my gentle reader,
Whose apprenticeship in the arts of Satrapy
Won't come about for a while. But don't
Worry, reader, just go ahead and enjoy
The poem. They'll never make me laureate
And they'll never give you what you
Think you deserve. When they make you
The Satrap of Alexandria, Kansas,
Maybe you'll connive with the plebs to
Get me a reading that pays enough
For my trip and a couple of beers.

ALEXANDRIAN KINGS

They are little kings of little kingdoms,
But why not celebrate them anyway.
Here comes Caesarion and his
Little brothers, Alexander and Ptolemy.
Why deny them some pomp as it
All means so little now. Notice the
Handsome soldiers who make up
A parade but could never fight a war.

Alex, how about Armenia?
Tolly, what about Cilicia for you?
And Caesarion, we'll deck you with
Flowers, tie bright ribbons in your hair.
You can be our king of kings.

In the great stadium the citizens were
Led in cheers—*hip, hip, Harrah,* that
Sort of thing. And they sang that song
About the fellows being, what was it,
Ah yes—"*Jolly Good.*" I may have skipped
A century or two; as a scribe, I'm given
To looking forward rather than back.

Oh, but they cheered in Greek, not English,
They cheered, some of them, in Egyptian
And Hebrew. Bring us King Faruk, dig us
The Suez Canal. Let's praise the fat kings
Of the fat nations. Is there a thin Jew
At the table? Is the laughter coming from
T.E. Lawrence and Lawrence Durrell?

PHILHELLENE

I know the only thing that's really Greek
Near where I live is a greasy spoon diner
Called Zorba's. Of course Zorba doesn't
Run the place—Jim Sweeney does—
But they can make you a kebab and
Pour you a beer. But about my commission.
Make me look like I own the neighborhood,
But still have a sympathetic face. Give me
A warm smile, make me look like someone
Who might have been an artist but instead
Went into business. "Sweeney the Greek"
They call him. Funny don't you think? Two
More blocks and we're there. I'll pay
You after I see what you do. Most guys
These days just have a photograph. But I
Want more than that. And underneath
The image I want you to print very clearly
In Greek: *Philhellene*. Practice the alphabet
Now and then before you get there or
You'll botch it. By "get there" I mean by the time
The rest of the Portrait is done. *Philhellene*
Comes last. The Romans taking over the
Streets around here will be impressed.
You ready for a kebab? That's Jimmy
Himself standing by the door.

YES OR NO

Today is one of those days when someone
Must say grandly Yes or greatly No. These are not
Days marked on any calendar, but kept secret
In the mind of shifty Hermes until he deigns to
Reveal them at the last possible moment.

The man getting up in the morning has only
One leg in his pants when he is called upon.
Yes he says, tripping over his cuffs and making
His lover (who is still in bed) laugh at him.
My darling one, she says, you have said grandly Yes
Tripping over your trousers. Perhaps you should
Have said greatly No.

                  Meanwhile, the man outside the city
In a small encampment is called on by Hermes as well.
No, he says, thundering. He is lucky to be fully dressed
When Hermes puts to him the question. Why should
He say, greatly, No? He must say greatly No because
The grand Yes is now stuck in the trouser leg of the
The affirmer in the town. The letters cut into his thigh.

THE DISPLEASURE OF THE SON OF SELEUCUS

Ptolemy Peters arrived in our part of town
In a mess. He was an embarrassment
To all Alexandrians, even those of us who
Had moved away and taken new names.
He had only three slaves and he, like them,
Was barefoot. We feared he'd make a
Mockery of all his former countrymen
If anyone knew. Demetrius—now he
Called himself "Dean" and was the son
Of Seleucus but didn't let on—"Dean"
Whispered to Ptolemy, "Kid from now on
You're 'Pete'; and don't act like you
Know us. At least you might have found
Yourself a pair of shoes and a fresh
Shirt, maybe even a tie. The Romans
In this part of town let you pretend to
Be Satraps in yours, so at least dress
To the part. And if you don't have any
Pretty clothes for your slaves then wait
Until you do. These three look like
Common tarts." "Dean" is so worried
That he slips away for an hour and
Returns from the habadish man with

Duds he's bought with coins stolen from
Seleucus. He gently wraps a purple robe
Over Pete's narrow shoulders; he puts
Rings on his fingers, a hat on his head.
Unfortunately, the shoes don't fit. But
Never mind—they are clearly new and
Pete can pretend he carries a pair
Because he doesn't want the bright shine
To collect mud from the street (for it
Had recently rained and the street
In this part into town has yet to be
Paved). "Now then Ptolemy Peters,"
Whispers Dean—"I mean, that is,
New Neighbor Pete, you maybe begin
To resemble the New Greek Alexandrian,
With fitting clothes and an unpretentious
Name instead of some beggar aiming to
Present himself to The Leader for alms.
Meanwhile, you can sell your slaves
To me who will dress them up and put
Them on the market as Holy Prostitutes
Come from a country that only I have
Visited, one lacking Satrap or any kind
Of local chief, but full of beautiful girls."

THE HEIRS OF DARIUS

The Poet Laureate is writing a poem in praise
Of the Leader. That's what they pay you for
He thinks. But what of merit has this leader
Achieved? The poet can think of nothing. Still,
By midday he must present a finished poem
In the Leader's oval office and, worse, read
It aloud to a group of dignitaries. Why has
The leader failed at what he set out to do?
Was it the Russians? Was it the Chinese? It
Is too early for troubles with China or Russia.
He Recalls that he writes in Cappadocia, that
His leader is merely son of a Satrap known
To the plebs as Thecamelhumpman, though
Compared by his courtiers to his great
Forbear Darius and hailed as Dionysus
And Eupator! The Laureate will get the last bit
into his poem. What everyone remembers
Is an unfortunate scandal, to cover which
Even Dionysus and Eupator must function
Mainly as diversion. Did I say he is writing
In Greek? He is writing in Greek. How many
Cappadocians will be able to read him? But
Only one reader matters to him, The Leader
Himself, descendent of

I looked away for a moment and he was gone,
Leaving behind what we have here

My comments on his now unfinished work.

During that same moment when I looked away a war
with Rome began. Legions attacked the Cappadocians
who struggled to resist. Poets who wrote in any language
but Latin hid under their desks. The Laurate had
intended to explain the failures of his Leader by blaming
all his enemies, especially the Romans. And behold!
The mere thought of that gambit conjured the Romans
themselves. There they were. Get under your desk. Run
for your life. Those who did neither got used to the
Roman rule, but made it a point not to mention Darius,
Mithridates, or even Dionysus and Eupator in certain
contexts. So here I am back at work, not a poet of course,
let alone someone "hailed" as anything much, doing my
job of annotating unfinished works. Yesterday it was the
Romans, but tomorrow they say it will be the Barbarians,
and that means I live with my packed suitcase beside me,
ready to flee. I'll leave behind no statement of Farewell,
but I can tell you that for a little joke on them all I've
changed the poem in such a way that it now

IN A SMALL TAVERN

It was the middle of the night
And we had been talking
Well beyond closing time, though
Talking mainly with gestures
Because he did not know Greek.
The small round table far to the back
Of the tavern contained the several
Bottles, half full of the local red that
The sleeping waiter had not taken away.

It was hot, and late, and I could smell
The sweat of his armpits. His shirt
Was unbuttoned and not tucked in
His trousers. I believed him to be one
Of those British soldiers, come so far
To chase German tanks across the desert
At one point he put his foot in my groin.
I knew the Brits had waterboarded
A tank commander that afternoon.
The thought gave me a kind of thrill.
Why not drown for the motherland?
My own motherland was under occupation.
Here we were, both in Egypt. I said to him
In Greek, "Open your mouth," opening my own
So he'd know what I meant. I leaned toward

Him and with my palm pushed back his
Forehead, which he permitted without any
Kind of objection. He half reclined leaning

On the back of the chair, head back, mouth
Hanging open. I pulled the cork from a bottle
And poured the entire contents down his
Throat as he gagged and spluttered and spat.
The Brits had not used wine on the German
Tank commander. When my friend had
Recovered, he stood, brushed himself off,
And said, in English, "Thank you." As the waiter
Comes to clean the table I rise and look him

In the eye, remember that he is my countryman
And made a fair profit from the war. I come
Here every night. But the night I have just spoken
About, that was more than thirty years ago. He
And I are both getting old. I am generally regarded
As a harmless and reclusive poet. But I used to
Follow Arab boys down dark streets in the night, or
Come here for my wine, hoping that someone might
Join me. As that man did of whom I have spoken.

APOLLONIUS

Some citizens still believe in his miracles,
Those of Apollonius, though he has been away
For a long time now. Those who saw
The miracles have died or become senile,
So what should we believe? I know a poet
Who believes that he'll return from wherever
He has gone in order to restore to us
The Greek gods of antiquity. And a philosopher
Has written a book all about him. There was
A reported sighting as far off as Ephesus.
Perhaps he goes about in disguise and laughs
At our speculations. Perhaps he understood
That he wasn't really needed. Those of us who
Are Christian go to church and are nostalgic
For the reign of pious Justin. Still, it's a large
Congregation where not only idolators but even
An idol or two would never be noticed.

ACHILLES' HORSES

Zeus was sad when he heard the horses
Of Achilles weep. After all, they had first of all
Belonged to him. But why weep for hubristic
And vain Patroclus? Ah, because he was
Achilles' friend. They shake their manes and
Paw the ground. Their tears are the size
Of pearls. Immortal, they don't know what
To do among these mortal men. Achilles
Seems unwell, rages, even looks at them,
The beautiful white horses, with some kind
Of accusation in his eyes. But they drew
No chariot of that proud boy the Trojan killed.
If they had, Patroclus would have lived—
But somewhere else, somewhere far from
The field of slaughter, a place where things
And men and horses all fall upward and
Where no one's anything falls down. This
Is so difficult for men to understand—that
There is such a place—that the horses
Weep for ignorance of men even more than
For their deaths. Three times round the
Citadel sets no clock for them. It neither
Winds nor unwinds anything. Achilles' horses
Very soon will fall up all the way to Zeus.

Don't cry, they'll say; we're back. When Zeus
Unstraps the chariot, God and horses walk
Together and away. And away from away.

THE WORST

You prepare for the worst,
Spending your days in anticipation,
Practicing ways to avoid it. You're sure
You know the form it will take.

But something different comes at you
And it's worse than the worst, and it
Takes an unexpected form, and you are
Unprepared. Your candles are already lit.

III

HOMAGE TO PETER TAYLOR BY WAY OF GEORGE GARRETT

DOUBLE OR TRIPLE VISION, PETER TAYLOR, GEORGE GARRETT, ETC.

Peter Taylor, *Complete Stories*, vols. 1 and 2, Library of America; Hubert H. McAlexander, *Peter Taylor: A Writer's Life*, Louisiana State University Press; George Garrett, *Double Vision*, University of Alabama Press.

I've always liked books of verse that included some prose. I could cite a number of precedents, but I started doing this early myself, with my first volume of poetry, *Bucyrus*. One section of that book was a kind of incantatory fiction. Other books have included essays, either in the middle or at the end, and my longer poems themselves have almost always modulated into and out of prose passages somewhere along the line.

I find that I have never written about Peter Taylor before. I do so here with the help of George Garrett in ways that you're about to see. Many of my essays in books of prose have been intended to bring attention to neglected writers. Peter Taylor, alas, now falls into that category, in spite of his long and prolific career. The same cannot be said about Marcel Proust, subject of another essay toward the end of this book, but it probably can be said about Donald Justice, certainly about Justice's fiction. In a way, Justice plays the part with regard to Proust that Garrett does with regard to Taylor. Or at least one could look at it that way.

And so—

How to write an essay about a man writing a review in a novel? Such ephemera. The man in the novel writes the review about an actual person, the novelist and storywriter Peter Taylor, and he himself is an actual person, George Garrett, the novelist and poet. Garrett lived next door to Taylor in Charlottesville, Virginia, for ten years or so. His assignment is to write 800–1000 words about Hubert McAlexander's biography of Garrett's former neighbor called *Peter Taylor: A Writer's Life*, published three or four years after Taylor's death.

I've read the biography myself. I was drawn to it because, many years ago, Taylor was my teacher at Ohio State University. The book by George Garrett is called *Double Vision*. It was recommended to me by Thomas McGonigle, a phrase from whose essay "The Writer's Life" is quoted in Garrett's book: "the dead are always with us." McGonigle is author of *St. Patrick's Day*, winner of the 2016 Notre Dame Review Book Prize. I'm an editor of *Notre Dame Review*. When I was in Columbus a year ago, visiting Ohio State, I met the poet

Nin Andrews, author of *Our Lady of the Orgasms*. This version of Our Lady is not celebrated at Notre Dame, where I taught for fifty years. But more to the point, Nin Andrews told me that her father was Peter Taylor's "best friend," and that they often met over drinks to tell each other stories. Some of her father's stories became, in print, Peter Taylor's stories. I once told Peter Taylor a story as well. He laughed and laughed but, as far as I know, never wrote it up. He told me that he thought my poetry was better than my fiction. That made me sad, as I had wanted to write a great American novel. But he was right. He asked me what poets I was reading. Yeats and Eliot, I said. He said he meant contemporary poets. I wasn't reading any contemporary poets. He told me I ought to look up his Kenyon roommate. "Who's that?" I asked. He said his Kenyon roommate was Robert Lowell. It was 1959 and *Life Studies* had just been published. Out I went and bought a copy at Long's Bookstore, Columbus. It changed my life. In the end, everything gets tangled up with everything else.

In *Double Vision* George Garrett and Peter Taylor get tangled up with the fictional doppelgängers Frank Toomer and Aubrey Carver. Toomer, like Garrett, is suffering from double vision brought on by the neurological condition called Myasthenia Gravis. (I know a good deal about that as I did a lot of research about it when my wife was misdiagnosed with the condition some years ago.) Toomer lives next door to Carver, a writer only a decade older than himself, as Garrett lived next door to Taylor. When Garrett finds it difficult to write about himself and Taylor, he switches to Toomer and Carver. That sounds like a bit of contrived postmodern machinery, but it's not. Toomer and Carver allow the author to say things about Garrett and Taylor that he couldn't have said without recourse to the doubles. As for the review itself, Toomer is unable in the end to write his piece on the biography of Carver, and chapter 27 prints his apologetic letter to Colin Walters, books editor of the *Washington Post*. On the other hand, Garrett not only manages to write his review of Hubert McAlexander's *Peter Taylor: A Writer's Life* but also prints it as it appeared in the *Washington Post*. This is a novel obviously full of play and games, but it is also very moving, especially for anyone who knew Peter Taylor or admires his work. For example, in a paragraph like this:

> I paused from my efforts and read again some of
> my favorite short stories by Peter Taylor for the
> first time in many months, rejoicing in them even
> as I felt a heavy sense of loss and sorrow for the
> man and for his art. The contemporary American
> habit of ranking everything—the best living
> sculptors, the five worse-dressed formalist poets in
> the Western world—is utterly contemptible. But

somewhere above and beyond all that foolishness
all that expense of spirit and of common sense
there are a precious few who are simply inimitable
and therefore irreplaceable. *Peter, we miss you.*

So: I knew Taylor, though a very long time ago, and I
have admired his work ever since I read some of it as an
undergraduate. I am now roughly the age Taylor was when
he died. Garrett thinks of his work as a "geezer novel," and
in fact uses the distressing word "geezer" again and again.
He was old when he wrote it, and Taylor had died. So
had an entire generation of writers, the contemporaries of
both men, and the book is an elegy for that generation—
perhaps the last one able to take something like a vibrant
literary culture for granted. As we watch "literary fiction"
dying off through the course of the narrative—a situation
where John Grissom becomes a villain and Robert Pinsky
reading poems on TV a joke—we realize that the literary
generation to which Garrett, Taylor, Toomer, and Carver
belong is, also, the last of the writers to have fought in
World War II or Korea, after which the norm became
"small war / on the heels of small war," as Robert Lowell
wrote.

Carver, Garrett reveals, had a naval career during
which he suffered constant illness and absolute terror on

convoy escort ships always vulnerable to torpedoes fired from German submarines. He never writes a word about these experiences and only speaks about them to the few friends who would understand—like Toomer. Garrett, who, like Toomer, was in Korea as an enlisted man and who wrote a biography of James Jones, author of *From Here to Eternity* and *The Thin Red Line*, knows from the biography he is reading, if not from Taylor himself, that his neighbor shipped as sergeant first to Northern Ireland during World War II, and then to a camp near London. Following the Normandy invasion and the Battle of the Bulge, Taylor escaped active fighting on the continent when, due to a minor scandal involving his commander, the order for a deployment in which he would have been included was unexpectedly rescinded. On V-E Day, he was still in London, "reading the works of Trollope" and writing "Allegiance," in which an American soldier visits an expatriate aunt in England and "feels [himself] still a prisoner in [his mother's] parlor at Nashville." As he prepared to return home, he was on the verge of writing some of his best early work.

*

At this point, as I write, there is a heavy *thunk* on my front porch. It's the delivery I've been waiting for—two gorgeous volumes in the Library of America series, Peter Taylor's *Complete Stories*—volume 1: 1938–1959 and volume 2: 1960–1992. So: Taylor is canonized in the American Plèiade. But is he read? Not by many. Taylor, who was once revered as "the American Chekhov" and whose earlier volume of *Collected Stories* was called by Joyce Carol Oates "one of the major works of our literature," gets somehow lost among other Southern writers, all of them women more or less of his generation, when most readers choose stories by Eudora Welty, Carson McCullers, Flannery O'Connor, or Katherine Anne Porter over his own. Among post-Faulkner males, he may be remembered as a junior member of the Southern Agrarians who taught him—Ransom, Tate, and Penn Warren. Once he got to the University of Virginia as writer-in-residence, he actually lived in a house once owned by Faulkner himself. He must have felt the burden of that. But I knew him, not in the South, but in the Midwest, where he came to Ohio State during a brief period itself interrupted by a year in Paris, about which he wrote one of his best stories, "Je Suis Perdu." Among other things, that beautiful story is about a writer who has come to Paris too late—too late in the century, and too late in his own life. He is no longer thirty, and it is no longer the 1920s. But what did he do to deserve Columbus, Ohio? (As for me, I was born there, so I had no choice.)

The first thing I do with the vast number of pages in the LOA edition is to scan both the table of contents and the notes to discover what Taylor actually wrote when he was in Columbus—on the east side of town, to be exact, in Bexley, where some of the old money and the two prestigious private schools resided at the time. As far as I can make out, there is only one story written in Columbus and about Columbus, "At the Art Theater," a short piece rejected, as many others were soon to be, by the *New Yorker*, with which journal he continued to have a "first reading" agreement and whose bankrolled largesse allowed him to ask for $1,000 on a fairly regular basis even when he wasn't doing his best writing and when the editors began thinking he might even be something of a liability, a genteel white southern gentlemen who, like the Agrarians, had a disturbing nostalgia for the Old South and whose black characters were mostly servants or ancient retainers among some old households, almost apparitions living in and around the old Logan place in "Miss Leonora When Last Seen." Anyway, I open volume 2 to "At the Art Theater."

With a shock of recognition I find both the characters and myself at the arts cinema on the edge of Ohio State University. The "state university" is not identified as OSU, but anyone who has grown up in Columbus would recognize both the setting and the specific movie theater. During the late 1950s and early 1960s I spent almost as much time at this cinema as I did at Marty's 502, the local jazz club. This was, after all, the great era of international avant-garde cinema, and literary types of my own generation loved all of it—from Bergman and Fellini to Antonioni and Godard. In the story, an engaged couple have just seen a Bergman film; Taylor doesn't say which one. The girl, a professor's daughter, gets it, or at least thinks she does; her fiancé does not. Outside, after the showing, they meet an acquaintance (from Bexley), who has found the whole thing "creepy." The professor's daughter is annoyed by the Bexley girl's response; the boyfriend is secretly sympathetic. In fact, there's not much more to the story than that, except that Taylor tells us that the disagreement regarding Bergman prefigured a bad marriage. This might all seem a little exaggerated, except that I had almost the same experience at the same art cinema at the same time. In my case the professor's daughter was the skeptical viewer and I, although certainly no sophisticated film buff, saw something in Bergman that immediately separated me from the world that my girlfriend inhabited. I might well have married her; but I did not. I'm not boasting about my superior sensibility; in other matters she was way ahead of me. But she didn't get Bergman, and not getting Bergman turned out to be important.

I doubt that Taylor remembered me as an undergraduate student at OSU. His Hubert McAlexander tells us that Taylor found his Ohio State students "the worst he had ever taught." As for the city, Taylor said in a letter at the time that he and his wife "hate Columbus. I really think another year is all we'll be able to take of it. Everything is so damned dull." I certainly understand and sympathize. During Taylor's "Je Suis Perdu" year in Paris, he wrote to my undergraduate advisor, Albert Kuhn, saying that he would not be returning to the university for the next academic year. I expressed some upset about this to Kuhn since I had already enrolled in Taylor's creative writing class and was looking forward to it. Kuhn said, "I think Taylor will change his mind. Let's keep you enrolled." As it turned out, Kuhn was correct. Within weeks Taylor wrote to OSU saying that he had made a bad decision and wanted, if possible, to reverse it. To a nineteen-year-old "radical" like me, this seemed an act of cowardice. I was torn. I wanted to take his class, but I was also thinking, "if the guy had any guts he'd stay in Paris." When I in fact showed up in his class, I was in a fairly aggressive state of mind. Why couldn't he be like Hemingway and Fitzgerald? Who needs a job? Who has any children or needs to pay a mortgage? Who would actually choose to live in Columbus? I actually had a copy of Roth's *Goodbye Columbus* in my book bag. I intended to put it on my desk, in full view of the other students. But then Peter Taylor started to talk.

It has been said of his fiction that much of it derives from the oral tradition, that one hears a speaking voice more than a writerly style in his major works. I think that's very true. After a few months listening to Taylor talk in class, I finally condescended to read some of the stories that had won prizes, especially the great "Venus, Cupid, Folly and Time" (which I read in the *Kenyon Review*, the *New Yorker* having rejected it). There he was, just like at some parties I attended, *telling a story*. I remember telling my girlfriend—the same one who went with me to the Bergman film—that "it sounds just the way he talks in class." Beyond recognizing the voice, however, I didn't have a clue what was going on. The allegory escaped me entirely, and the setting just seemed "creepy," as the Bexley girl had said of the Bergman film. I was, truth to tell, frightened by "Venus, Cupid, Folly and Time" in ways I couldn't explain to myself. I read the whole thing aloud to my girlfriend who said, "I don't get it." I didn't get it either this time, but I was of course unwilling to admit it. I'm not sure I get it now. I'm going to read it again in the LOA edition very soon. Perhaps canonization will make for clarity.

Meanwhile, those several years we were both at Ohio State. Poor Taylor had not too long before managed to get tangled up in some unpleasant academic politics when he was at Kenyon. (That's what his story "Dean of Men" deals with.) At OSU, the Sixties began to dawn in a number of ways that tossed that huge institution into turmoil. The Fair Play for Cuba Committee brought a speaker to town who was locked out of the building where he was meant to give his talk. There were demonstrations and, eventually, a faculty meeting called in order to censure the OSU president, Novice Fawcett (a wonderfully apt name) for abridging free speech on campus. I remember vividly a cartoon in the student paper, *The Lantern*, which showed a water faucet turning off the current of free speech. Following Fawcett's lockout of the building where the talk was to have been given, the administration packed the faculty meeting by calling in all of the agricultural specialists from branch campuses around the state and outvoted the actual Columbus faculty. This outcome broke up a very fine English Department, many of whose members went to California the next year. In fact, I was taught by some of the same people at Stanford that I had been taught by at OSU. At the end of this tumultuous period, I went to see Taylor in his office. He asked me where I was going. I said I was going West, and asked him where he was going. He said: "I'm going South," and he did.

Taylor was not very political, which is another reason his reputation declined shortly after he left Ohio State. And he was not, on the face of it, very experimental during a later period when the rising star at the *New Yorker* was Donald Barthelme. But it was certainly right for Taylor at that point to have headed back to his roots. There he found the support of people like his old friend Randall Jarrell at the University of North Carolina and, when he ended up at Virginia, George Garrett. Even at southern universities, however, his political attitudes were, well, conservative—and quite aggressive toward "liberal" colleagues even in Charlottesville, of all places, where there couldn't have been many of these. As he wrote in a letter,

My opinion of them gets lower every year. It is they who are responsible for all the upheaval in universities now. They love excitement, because they are timid men and it is the only excitement they have; and they love all the attention to academic life because it makes them seem important. They love the image of themselves as bold revolutionaries, yet they have chosen a very protected life, and how they cherish their tenure!

Then there were the crazies, the suicides, and the alcoholics—Lowell, Jarrell, Delmore Schwartz, John Berryman, Elizabeth Bishop, along with their students, Sylvia Plath and Anne Sexton. In this madhouse, Taylor was the one everybody counted on for sanity and stability, and he tried to provide that for both old friends and young students. At this late stage, it is distressing just to list the names. Madness and suicide had become fashionable. Taylor was perfectly aware of the dark side of things, wrote story after story in which the reader, at the end, realizes that he is sinking in quicksand. But Taylor began to be rejected, even by fellow *New Yorker* authors like John Updike, for stirring up "tempests in teapots." Was Updike envious? He has many teapots of his own to account for. Taylor's tempests were real enough, and all of the teapots were broken.

"Venus, Cupid, Folly and Time" is chronologically framed by two autobiographical stories—"1939," about a trip Taylor and Lowell made from Kenyon to New York on the eve of World War II, and that rare story with a foreign setting, the previously mentioned "Je Suis Perdu." The former, published in 1954, probably influenced Lowell in *Life Studies* with its willingness to exploit the lives of both the author and his friends (and their girlfriends or wives). Lowell was at first offended by the piece, but later admired it. Also, Lowell could not have missed the warning to the autobiographically inclined with implications as much for himself as for Taylor:

> picture me for just a moment—much changed
> in appearance and looking at you through gold-
> rimmed spectacles—behind the lectern in a
> classroom. I stand before the class as a type of
> writer whom Trollope might have approved
> . . . . this . . . is a man who seems happy in the
> knowledge that he knows—or thinks he knows—
> what he is about. And from behind his lectern
> he is saying that any story that is written in the
> form of a memoir should give offense to no one,
> because before a writer can make a person he has
> known fit into such a story—or any story, for
> that matter—he must do more than change the
> real name of that person. He must inevitably do
> such violence to that person's character that the
> so-called original is forever lost to the story.

A better-known passage came all but posthumously in Lowell's "Epilogue" to his last book, *Day by Day*:

> . . . sometimes everything I write
> with the threadbare art of my eye
> seems a snapshot,

lurid, rapid, garish, grouped,
heightened from life,
yet paralyzed by fact.
All's misalliance.
Yet why not say what happened?
Pray for the grace of accuracy
Vermeer gave to the sun's illumination
stealing like the tide across a map
to his girl solid with yearning.
We are poor passing facts,
warned by that to give
each figure in the photograph
his living name.

George Garrett must have heard both of these passages, or something like them, talking to him when he sat down to write *Double Vision*. Taylor's warning, or something like it, is responsible for the creation of Frank Toomer and Aubrey Carver. Lowell's lament, or something like it, is responsible for Toomer and Carver reverting regularly to Garrett and Taylor. The vision is double, the emotions ambivalent, and the style an attempt to reconcile mixed feelings.

Garrett did not meet Taylor until the Charlottesville period when he lived in a house first acquired by Taylor and right next door to the larger Taylor home. Houses meant a lot to Taylor. He bought and restored many; sold some at a profit; lived sometimes in several at once. He had a near obsession about them. What I think of as his one revenge story, "Dean of Men," is driven by his outrage of having been deceived and manipulated by colleagues at Kenyon out of the house there he wanted to live in. I'm surprised that none of his books were titled by the name or location of a house, some adult version of *A House at Pooh Corner*. Anyway, living in a small Taylor house and next door to a large one, Garrett invented his doubles.

I'm told by McGonigle—"the dead are always with us"—that Garrett always referred to "Mr. Taylor," not "Peter." I understand and approve. By the end of my teaching career, when I was over seventy, my students automatically called me "John" and referred to my wife and me as "you guys." These assumed liberties make one nostalgic for old formalities. Even back in high school we were addressed by our teachers and called each other by our surnames. We were Matthias, Goss, Barkan, Whitaker, Brown. When I started teaching, once we had women in classes at Notre Dame, they were Miss Barton, Miss Cecil, Miss Wolfe (and now and then a Sister Immaculate or two). I liked that. Would I at eighteen have called Mr. Berryman "John"? It's unthinkable. Peter Taylor's family called him Pete. He nixed that upon his arrival at Kenyon.

If you want to diminish greatness, blast it with the given names or nicknames reserved only for the closest friends. An Eliot hater at one of TSE's American readings accosted the poet and said, "I didn't catch the name." Understanding well what was afoot, Eliot said his name was "Tom." "Oh," said the detractor, "are you English?" Tom said, "No, I'm from St. Louis."

So: Mr. Taylor. That's what I called him as well. And when I got lost in the "Venus" story, I had no idea what I should call him the next day. I had spent half a term listening to his genial comments on our miserable stories, which he read aloud in class as we all, anonymous author and his classmates, squirmed. To make things even more embarrassing, when he came to an obscenity or a expletive, he said "bleep." Tough guys were so humiliated by this that they stopped writing tough guy stories entirely. But Taylor's "Venus" story knew more about the world of erotic excess, including incest, than any of his students ever imagined.

That story, written in Bexley and published while Taylor was briefly living in Italy, is probably one of the best short fictions ever written by an American. Randall Jarrell hated it. The *New Yorker* turned it down. I am not going to summarize it here because I want to tempt readers to get hold of Taylor's LOA edition and read it. The editor, Ann

Beattie, gives it the attention that it warrants in her intro-
duction. Only three or four other Taylor stories compete
with it for top billing—perhaps "The Old Forest," "Miss
Leonora When Last Seen," and "In the Miro District."

*

I have just returned from another trip to Columbus
after a visit to see my daughter and her family who are now
living there. I tried to find the Lane Ave. Arts Cinema,
but of course it is gone. There is an organization called
Ohioana Library, specializing in books by Ohio authors.
At their annual book fair, I asked many "Ohio authors"
if they read Peter Taylor. Only one person remembered a
story he thought he had read in a high school short fiction
anthology. "Ohio authors" know about their contempo-
raries. I was asked if I meant "Tyler." Perhaps I'd have
had better luck in Nashville or Memphis or St. Louis, but
maybe not. My two former students who teach at Ohio
State both now work in film studies. I was told by one
of them, "it's almost impossible to get students to read."
But "creative writing" evidently thrives. The students are
keen to write, but not to read. I asked one of my former
students what his students write about. "A lot of them
write about movies."

When Miss Leonora was last seen, she was leaving Thomasville for one of her obsessive jaunts around the countryside that she begins making when her ancestral house, Logana, is scheduled to be demolished to make way for a new school. She drives only at night and spends her days as a guest at a series of old-fashioned tourist homes run by widows, retired farmers, and other kinds of locals. The main object of her Logan forebears was to keep Thomasville a kind of private fiefdom and picturesque town sheltered even from new roads and railways. Thomasville is a kind of local colorist's parody village, a Southern version of Garrison Keillor's Lake Wobegone. When Taylor left Columbus at the urging of Randall Jarrell and took up a job at a branch of the University of North Carolina he was happy at the prospect of homecoming, but must also have known that he was also taking risks. When "last seen" in Columbus, he was politely saying goodbye, but also, under his breath, good riddance.

Was Taylor in danger of becoming just a Southern "regional" writer? To some extent, the answer must be yes, and his region became a kind of triangle with points at Nashville, Memphis, and St. Louis. If one were determined to misunderstand him, one might say, like Miss Leonora, that he "was determined to populate [the region] with the sort of people [he] thought should live there." After the move south to North Carolina and, later, Virginia, there were to be no more stories set in Paris or London or even Columbus. Although his master was Henry James, not William Faulkner, his region was in fact claimed as a fictive reality in the same way that Faulkner claimed Yoknapatawpha County as "sole owner and proprietor." He didn't, in fact, write about "the sort of people he thought should live there," but about the sort of people who broke down the order of things in his special kingdom, and those who threatened the Old South about which his ambivalence produced ambiguous figures of all kinds, the incestuous pair in "Venus, Cupid, Folly and Time" being as representative as any other.

It was a good thing for literature that Taylor ended up living next door to George Garrett. And also that he helped hire the young Ann Beattie (only twenty-five) to teach with him at the University of Virginia, for she is the editor of these two magnificent volumes. She clearly loves the work and the memory of the man. So do I. In a more civilized time, Peter Taylor would have been a popular author, like Trollope himself. Since his death, the times have only gotten worse. It is very difficult for me to imagine an audience for these books at the present moment. Taylor had no desire to be "a writer's writer." After all, he published in the *New Yorker* whenever he could. I wonder how receptive that journal would be to his work now. And, if not in the *New Yorker*, where would he publish? Although he wrote three novels, one of them, *A Summons to Memphis*, a Pulitzer Prize winner, his major achievement was as a short story writer. He loved "telling stories." I envy the uninitiated lucky few who will pay the (rather considerable) cost of these volumes. They will be reading an American master for the first time, and they will be getting a bargain. Joyce Carol Oates was right: these stories are "one of the major works of our literature."

IV

HOMAGE TO HACHESTON HALT AND OTHER STOPS

J.B. AND E.P.

"Hugh Selwyn Mauberley" and
"Homage to Mistress Bradstreet"
Are both nearly perfect works.
Finishing either, we are clearheaded
Quickwitted, pleased & informed.

The Cantos and *The Dream Songs*
Are a mess. Brilliant fragments
Emerge, all with sharp elbows,
Clenched fists and kicks in the groin.
We never finish them. We weep.

JUST SHORT POEMS

(for Anthony Walton, who asked for some)

I. For A.W.

Just short poems
or short just poems,
the justice in the
duration or the law?
Justice, they say, must
be seen to be done.
But length does also
matter. Terms and
temperament matter.
Judicial temperament,
what's that? A phrase
to praise a judge. But
long or short terms?
What do you say
Your Honor, Mr. Felon?
These poems are only
misdemeanors, subject
to short terms, just
accusations, quick trials.
The question is, what
trails after? What trails
after are after-trials.

II. Found in My Mother's Bible

If I ever doubted
ever even doubted
if I doubted that the steps
ever doubted
steps taken and the
token stops and
starts of their powers
over me and what was mine
said powers said
of attorney turning
in regard to me but not
in my regard in regard
to the steps taken
that were wrong and
rights wrung
out of me without
regard to many doubts
without regard
without regard to many
reasons stated all
against the said powers and
my reasons stated more
than once my debts and
the deaths of many of
them since before and yet

the money never was
an issue and my reason sound
as theirs, then I

III. Doppler

doth affect us, doubles down
on us as waves narrow
and a sparrow falls from the sky.
So, dapple doppelgänger guy,
do gods notice the effect if one
means or if another ends?
Dapper was the bird that fell
as doubt made numbskulls of us all
while awaiting—at a crossing of
the kinds—a police car, train.
Gather all, Maintainer, everything
from inside out to outside in
if Indiana is your state and horn
or siren blare. There we
know the stipulated bloody drill:
eye confides whereas the ear
confounds and sounds like
Still will never measure silence.
I mean to say I cannot
stay at my own statutory post.
Past is posited as future and is
fortune's wave—*hi!* as we go buy.
Portion and your proposition
fall out of balance, mine too if
valence is all. In the fall the red

and yellow leaves. Snow verbs alas
and the queen of hearts is necessary
and your card. Credit it and call.
If the ayes have it, it's a pity that we
only vote with doppled ears.

IV. Bent or straightened, someone

. . . had rendered maister C. Élan's
Engführung not as *stretto* not
as *fugue* but as *Straightening* and
with yes, vegetation; yes, the
whirl of particles, and there was
time left, yes, or was it time
right and *center:* field as batten
down or batter up the yield as
someone scooped it, doubled pay,
and let it stay in play and straight
enough lost it in the leafy fall,
a tit for tat, the treaty that
a pretty punning girl & the spin-
ning planet morphed into a *whoosh!*
a strike zone or fast drone
a river run in tune. To render
what? The which of it!
the *wham!* The niche of history
is, naturally enough, later on.
A friend told me he had read
with Hamburger and Wieners at
an Ancel event, I think, for C. Élan:
tribute or a tribulation? When
he got home his son was the one
to say: *Hamburger & Wieners?*

Will that be with fries? His father so
with all poetry and languages
besotted in those young days we
all were blessed to share that
he didn't see, he didn't even hear
that it was funny. He was somewhere
else: in Hamburg or Weimar, Delft.
His son put It to him, straightened him
all out about the daft coincidence,
all out about the strange curves
in the nature of all things.

V. Music Room Gothic

Such a big house. Such a little boy.
There was even a music room to
which I sometimes went when all of
the adults were occupied. A piano was
there, but seldom played. Late autumn
sunlight poured through Victorian lace
over windows. Dust motes swarmed
in rivers of air. I would sit on the bench
and look at the keys. The adults were
somewhere down the long hallways,
off in distant rooms. I was alone.
Many doors were always locked. One
entire suite of rooms was blocked—
wooden panels nailed down the walls,
ceiling to the floor. In the attic loomed
a garish green table over which a famous
quarrel had occurred. Our visits became
fewer after that. I played black keys.
An uncle had told me: *If you only play
black keys you'll find that you make no
mistakes.* He was right, but I strayed.
I fell into the devil's mode, F and B
in the scale of C. I had already discovered
a "fifth," but this was something new,
a white key mischief, bad. Naughty boy,

I thought: You want to know about what
happens in those halls, those rooms.
Places where the keys unlock the faces
Frowning in the light of F and B in C.

HOMAGE TO HART'S CRANE ON THE MARRIAGE OF FAUSTUS AND HELEN

for Judge J. Manier

Fusty comes to mind around certain houses
In Ohio towns; but there might be a local bar
And a car or two rounding a pond where
Hart's crane stands on one leg and stares.

Stares at Helen, whose name puns so easily
With *Hell on*—for example, *hell on cities,*
Hell on ships, hell on cranes even, but whose
Fine Nuptials must be celebrated by the

Law that made Marlow, Goethe, and Mann.
Auden's Tom Rakewell was a pretty fusty
Faust, but we number him as well, as off he
Goes in the Auden libretto and Stravinsky's music.

Gounod danced a Faust for me in Paris
When I was a summer sophomore on my
Way to—where it does not matter now, for
I slept through both the opera and ballet—

But not Hart's crane. He didn't sleep. *Where's*

Helen? he honked (or squawked?) I knew
From my music class at school that Tom Rakewell
Married the ugliest woman in Europe in order

To prove that our choices are free. He didn't
Marry Helen or even Ann Truelove; alas
Poor Tom went mad. But Hart's father was
The man who invented *Life Savers*, the

Ubiquitous candy in everybody's pocket.
Somehow this confounded the son, who
Wrote about him *with smutty wings that flash
Equivocations*—which was really Byronic

Euphorian, falling before his time, child
(Harold) of Faust and Helen, trying to fly.
The crane shook his head; he'd known
All along that Euphorian was no Daedalus.

But where's Helen now? Gounod only gets as far
As Margherita's tale, interrupted by dance. The crane's
Not satisfied. And nor is Zeus, appearing as a swan,
Helen's winged and feathered dad.

And yes, I did digress

And jumped ahead as well. I thought
that cranes quacked or squawked.
When I paused back there with Rakewell, for
Research, I found that Cranes, well, bugle.

Crane's call is like a trumpet blast and can be heard
For miles. How I underestimated him. And this
Brass insult he splutters angrily at Swan,
Come to his daughter's wedding. Why would

Swann's daughter marry Faust, with
The ship of Menelaus almost in sight?
Where does Faust fit in? He too has a bugle
Call and a rattling good yarn to tell. He is

In fact, the very Hart of Crane. It was all
Understood from the beginning. Helen tricked
Her father, Leda, Menelaus, Paris, Agamemnon
And Odysseus. She was an Eidolon in Egypt

While the heroes on the beach fought about
An absence in the tower of Troy.
Faust bided his time. He knew it all. He'd have
To live through nonsense in a chapbook,

Oral tales, epics, plays and operas. He grew
Impatient, though, which led him to Mephisto.
What he'd been lacking was Hart's crane.
Who bugled, trumpeted: *The incunabula of*

The Divine grotesque, corymbulous formations
Spouting malice, plangent over meadows and
Empty houses like old women with teeth
Unjubilant. Now then honk or bray; be jubilant.

But was she concubine or wife? Menelaus got there
In one version of the tale. In another, he
Fails to arrive. Either way, the crane presides: Like
A marriage counselor, like a priest, like the

Phrase *I now pronounce you pain and strife.* It's
Possible. In our time, it's possible to be married or
Divorced in a court of law, and as everyone hurries
Through the centuries to the courtroom of my

Friend Judge Manier, the crane finds himself barred
From entering. No cranes allowed in the courtroom,
Or other birds. Was that original wager more of a
Plea bargain before the act? On everybody's part?

We'll never know. The crane resumes his residence
In the heart of the poet . . .

                              Or the poet

In the heart of the crane.

WITH A REFRAIN BY DENISE RILEY

Mop, mop, Georgette
And while you're at it don't forget
The others who on knees regret
The kind of life they'll never get
Mop, mop, Georgette

Mop, mop, Georgette
And see that you don't bitch & fret
About the rich who haven't yet
Failed to fetch deep sorrow's debt
Mop, mop, Georgette

Mop, mop, Georgette
You had no time to place a bet
Where wish was horse that always let
The rider win you never met
Mop, mop, Georgette

Mop, mop, Georgette
Mistress wants the floors all wet
While she lights a cigarette
And leaves you in her white Corvette
Mop, mop, Georgette

Mop, mop, Georgette
Remember you're a suffragette
A member of the soviet
And one day you will shout out *niet*
Mop, mop Georgette

Mop, mop, Georgette
But now you're in her kitchenette
Not to dance a minuet
But sweat with me through this duet
Mop, mop, Georgette

TILLS

       Un-
til that moment he had
trodden
only tentatively in the south
in the mind
indestructible

Till's son, and I remember hearing
Someone saying decades
later   *there are certain names that*
when you hear them simply
make you weep—

Anne Frank, Emmett Till

Perhaps not Ezra Pound, and yet
I do mean Ezra Loomis Pound
From Idaho
     among so many
dark faces sweating with him
near the Leaning Tower
when he wrote, that moment
leaning to his notebook—

and Till was hung today

(leaning from the hangman for
an instant but

hung.)

He was Lewis: Emmett Till's father—
evidence was worse than cir-
cumstantial
line in a Canto though
sing *until*

sung

FACEBOOK POST

A cat in spring light beside the winter shovel—
just a title for the photograph—but Michael posts
at once: *Good first line for a poem*. Maybe so, although
the photograph's a little out of whack. Then Terry
posts a question: *Which of these things does not
belong?* I think it must be the winter shovel since
the spring has come, but Terry says *No—it's the cat*.
I wonder why he thinks so. The cat, Clio, is bathed
in light, sleeping on a wicker chair before an east
window with a wide-open curtain. Her beauty blazes
at the center of all things. Take her away, and what's
left contains no life, just a small room full of objects:
hats on wall-hooks, the leaning shovel, the empty chair.
But when I put my finger over the cat I can see what
he means. The still life, where there is no life at all,
coheres entirely as a composition, but all's winter light,
haunting in its bleakness; the cat's been buried in
the cold earth outside, the shovel left against the wall.

HACHESTON HALT

for Diana

I was trying to remember what
It was called while telling
A friend who said you'd never lost
Your English accent that you'd
Never accepted American
Words for certain things either.
A boot was a boot (the trunk
Of a car), bobby pins were
Kirby grips, and your orders
For half-pints of cider or beer
Perplexed many a waiter or
The person you called the
Publican. Sometimes you'd
Exaggerate quite consciously—
As for example asking a grocer
Where you might find the
Mangelwurzels (sweet red beets).

But I was trying to remember
What you called the place where
The local train used to stop. By
The time I came to your Suffolk
Home it was no longer there.

We'd take a taxi from Ipswich.
The old connecting train used to
Stop for just a moment a few
Hundred yards from your country
Doorway, but hadn't done that
For years. You can't even get to
Aldeburgh or Deben by train
Anymore. In those early days
When the train did stop for
Your parents' guests to descend,
It was only for a minute—and
Your father would carry a set of steps
He'd raise up to the door so the
Friends didn't have to throw out
Their suitcase and jump. Then
I did remember, the very short stop
Was called Hacheston Halt.

I have beside me the Visitors' Book
From Cherry Tree. That was
The name of your house. In your
Small village, all the houses had names
Rather than numbers, and all but
A few faced on the street called the street.
The full address, a kind of poem I thought,
Was   Cherry Tree

Hacheston
Woodbridge
Suffolk

Woodbridge being inserted as it was
The closest town of any size. The first
name I recognize is Anthony Part in 1946,
and then a little later, in the same year,
Wayland Hilton-Young. Wayland was to
Become my brother-in-law in the 1960s
But I never met Anthony Part. I was
Told that he had joined the navy
Rather than the army to avoid the
Misfortune of being called Private Part.
In 1946 they'd still have come by train
To the halt, been met by Captain Adams,
Your recently retired father and led
Down the hill to what was then newly
Acquired: the Cherry Tree house
Made by joining together sometime
In the eighteenth century three small
Elizabethan cottages made of great
Beams and stuck together with the glue
Of local mud and horsehair.

The names go on: Frances Drury-Lowe
Elizabeth Hilton-Young, your half-sister

And Wayland's wife, Nigel Bonham-Carter,
Adam Paul, the local squire, and
Elizabeth Shakespeare, Duchess of
Bedford House. By now I'm up to 1953
And find Zbyszek Katarski, from
The White House, Parham. I once put
His name in a poem as being one of
The Polish airmen who stayed on in
The next village after the war. The airfield
Was up the hill a few hundred yards
Beyond the halt. It was a base for
B-17s which flew mainly American crews.
You can still walk the runways, though
They're full of grass and moss and weeds.
I flip ahead to the sixties, trying not to
Look at names of your other suitors who
Eventually came in flocks. At one point,
Your mother told me, you had four boyfriends
All named Michael and identified not by
Their surnames but by the number as they
Alternated in your affection: Michael 1,
Michael 2, Michael 3, and Michael 4.
I know there's a Russian and an Afghan
Boyfriend on the list, but rarely Englishmen,
Save for Richard Palmer, whom I met the
Very day I had to tell your father you were

Going to marry me and go off to America.
He fancied Richard Palmer for you and I
Even felt a little sorry for him when your
Mother gave him our good news.

I find my own first signature in June 1967,
And then again in 1971—we'd stayed
Away three years—and soon after that
The names of Cynouai and Laura, our young
Daughters, written in your hand. After that,
A steady stream of our own friends,
My mother, Lois, Joel and Sandy Barkan,
Vince Sherry and John Garvick, colleagues
Both of them, and then some early students,
All of those about as old as I am now.
There's a blank page, which I turn, and
There I find "Pam's Funeral Tea."
For me, your house became a Howards End
And Pamela, your mum, a Mrs. Wilcox.
Forster would have loved the place and
Early on, wasn't far away—living out his
Final years at King's College Cambridge.

Your mother told me that I had to ask
Your father for your hand, in "the traditional
Manner" she smiled. The old captain was

Quite deaf and hardly noticed that I
Was around on my several previous visits.
He'd sit in the summer house and smoke
His pipe between short bursts of work
In the garden. My job that morning had
Been to trim the hedge, so my hands
Were already shaking from holding the
Shears horizontally in front of me for
An hour. You were meant to be playing
Badminton with Richard Palmer who
Was sticking around a long time I thought.
Your mother even gave me a little push.
So up I walked to the open doors of
The summer house, a rotating affair
That could be turned to face the sun,
And stood there until the Captain
Looked up from his paper. I have no
Idea what I managed to say, but it
Was all a great surprise to him and
What he finally said was, "we'll see."
I nodded and went back to work on
Some weeds among the tomato plants.
Leaving Richard Palmer holding his racquet,
You and your mother came over to where
I dug and snipped on my knees. Which
Meant you did in fact find me in the

Traditional posture of a suitor for the hand
Of a maid. You bent down together and
Asked me what he'd said. I said he said
"We'll see," and you laughed. That's what
He always said, I was given to understand,
When he hadn't heard the question. He
Would not admit to being deaf. I would not
Admit not having asked him formally for
Your hand. Later there were longer
Conversations, and a private session in
The sitting room between the Captain
And his wife, the two of us having gone
For a walk, you said, "up by the halt."

So when I remembered Hacheston Halt,
The day when first it was pointed out
To me came swimming back to consciousness,
With all its humor and good luck. There
Seemed to be no Michaels standing jealously
On the narrow path, no Afghan or Russian,
And even Richard Palmer had left by
The time we returned. We had been reading
Poems by Edward Thomas earlier on
And you had his book in the pocket of
The apron you still wore. As we walked
Off Mrs Revel, the daily help, shouted

"Dinah, you've got your apron on." The
Family called you Dinah, and so of course
Did she. When we reached the narrow
Trench that had contained the rails, we
Sat on its edge, dangling our feet where
The train had run. You laughed and said
"It's almost like 'Aldestrop' that Thomas
Poem. Remember he wrote 'It was
Only a name, no one left the platform
And no one came.'" Thomas wrote that
The train had come "unwantedly" to
An empty platform. That was during the
War your father had fought. The trench
Your local train had run in looked for a
Moment sinister and dark. But this was
Not for long. And this was not at Aldestrop
And not a time of war. We were in luck.
We sat there swinging our feet at
Hacheston Halt.

V

HOMAGES TO SOME MASTERS AND SOME FRIENDS

THE MASTER READS TO
EDITH WHARTON

though with hesitation, just above a whisper, and,
she later said because she thought he was even then perhaps
in process of changing—his mind—and because,
she also said, he was doubtless moved by his own low voice

(or whispered hesitation) moving over syllables
making up this strange Other's even stranger song
of, he said, himself. Now that's ambiguous, she thought,
the song was not about the Master but about the self

proclaimed by this other self, American, Mr. Whitman, Walt.
Mrs. Wharton can't refrain from saying, during a short
but pregnant pause in this private (very) and unusual
searching recitation, But remember, Master, what you wrote

when you were young about the older, though not yet so
very old, Mr. Whitman, Walt. You said that his poems
showed the author's drab prosaic mind that only barely tried
(without success) to lift itself, she said he'd said, by

muscular effort, into poetry. There was no art, no measure,
in a word of it; there was no grace, no sense. The Master
bowed his head in momentary shame, and then read on while
also thinking, *an atrocity of youth, a deep disgrace* (his own)

as he now admires the words that he starts to read once more,
and even more reveres the memory of the man—strange, even,
as himself, though in a different (an opposite?) kind of way—for his
wound-dressing of the soldiers in the Civil War, his whispered

affection, his gifts of peppermints and cigarettes, his taking of
dictation from the dying of their last wills, their letters to
their mothers or beloveds, his—he says it to himself straight out—
muscular ability to love them and lift them high and up to death.

And now *he* was dying, now *he* went every other day to tend
the Belgians in the wards because so few of the nurses
spoke their language. *Languages!* he told them, and he could
only speak to those who didn't weep their Walloon tears

but just the French, as if the weeping were not language
in itself, as if the weeping could demand translation. But this
was not a day for which he'd signed up for in the wards, although
he'd gladly go if he were needed, if someone on the damned

machine—a telephone—told him that he was (if not very busy)
badly wanted because all the younger volunteers had failed
to arrive. He realized that he was staring at his friend, Mrs. W,
his dear old colleague, the one who paid the heavy bills for

a failed new edition of—she never said; he never knew—
his works. It was she who called him *Master*, though she
herself had mastered him in popular appeal and success,
and he savored it, thought his novels greater than her own.

But she didn't know that he was dying. He thought perhaps
that Whitman did. This poet of death, this nurse. He read
on in the endless poem. Mrs. Wharton was no Peter Doyle.
He'd read the letters Whitman wrote to him. So simple

and so plain. Mrs. Wharton was his colleague, not his
nurse. And benefactor, patron—no she'd never tell, not now—
and he'd have been embarrassed had he known. But this
moment held no question of embarrassment, but breath.

He couldn't breathe, not properly. Not the way one must
reciting (could it be?) great poetry. One day Americans
in early youth would read these elegies but only those who were
like Mrs. Wharton bother (damn it!) to read him. But there

was no one really *like* Mrs. Wharton. He hears her saying
that she'll now be off. She hopes he'll feel better soon.
He's vague about the time that's passed before he knows
that others gather round. He's now confused his reading

of another's poem with the dictation of his own original new
work to Miss Bosanquet, typist. He can see she's there, among
the others, standing by his brother's widow. How he'd
always argued with his brother who'd detested his late style.

No one knew what Pragmatism really was, so there!
If Mr. Walt were here what would *he* do now? He knew just what
a stroke felt like—a bolt of lightning launched by Zeus,
blasting through his brain, his mouth mouthing unmeaning

syllables and phonemes, floating free, tenses interchangeable,
genders all mixed up or somehow fused. *Live all you can*
he dictates to Miss Bosanquet, who writes it down, even though
she knows he long ago gave the line to Lambert Strether in

The Ambassadors. Des Vaeux is there and takes his pulse.
He thinks for a moment that his brother's widow may be
Mrs. Wharton, reads on to Miss Bosanquet who writes *What man
would whiten any sepulcher—a joke that Howells and I enjoyed*

*in reference to the suits that Mr. Clemens wore Mark Twain
it down to Whitman's Farewell My Fancy now that they've
not only given me a subject but also made me one I think I heard
you'd visited Verdun the battle field folded already into history*

this war the civil fellows fallen all upon each other bugger that
they say there in the wards and bugger this as well even the
Distinguished Thing he might have said Miss Edith meaning
you and certainly he'd not have called me anything but as

it were or as they say I'm British now but also still American
Vide or Cf. "The Jolly Corner"—not so bloody jolly was it—
told my brother I'd stay here I am Miss Bosanquet Miss Edith
Daisy Isabel and Minnie Constance Alice Mother Walt.

AFTER DOCTOR Z, PROFESSOR D

We miss him and his arguments, Professor D.
He argued? With himself. With others, too,
But, more importantly, he argued with himself,
As Yeats says a poet must. Otherwise, it's rhetoric—
And sometimes D served up a bit of that as well
In poems that were not always really poems. And didn't
Ever Doctor Z? The Russian whom Professor D
Inhabited, making his translations, roughly 1963–1965?

Amazing years, the sixties, for those arguments
With others or oneself. Pound–Ed Dorn and/or
Thomas Hardy–Larkin? Or/and Arthur Yvor Winters
And/or the giant Swedish Charles, rector of that
College called Black Mountain? Or chuck them out,
All of them, for Boris Pasternak? All on his own, or with
Akhmatova and/or Mandelstam, Tsvetaeva in Moscow
And/or Leningrad? Lovers of the (Slavic) word!

They wrote so far from Yorkshire, Cambridge,
Stanford, Nashville and the Grand Ole Opry.
I suppose he never went. To the opera (Grand Ole)
When he taught at Vanderbilt. But that was toward
The end, and he "heard Russian spoken" near what
Was the start of things for him. He wrote in his poem

About the war years in the Royal Navy stationed in
Archangel that he'd admit he was "enamored still."

Still: He was enamored still with Russian and
The sound of it. When he wrote the poem a long time
After. And yet before he'd ever seen Zhivago's poems
For lovely Lara. Half mad, sexually sea-born and/or
Snow-bound Larissa. From the sea, and wholly
Overwhelming. You'd leave your job for her, you'd
Leave your wife, your children, God. She gathered
To herself no tradition of a church. And yet Dissent.

Her dissent was of another kind than that of the English
Chapel. Wesley hymns, then, and/or Zhivago's poems?
The *and* of things no longer at that time working
In its and/or dialectic. Nearly dazed, amazed Professor D
Stared at the page where Y Zhivago turned into some
Kind of Jesus Christ himself, Lara into language-bride as
Sister Life. Goddamn the Moscow doctor's textament, its
Slippery slope of impure diction and erotic rage.

Still, it was perhaps a way out of something frozen.
A language he "could not command" spoke to an unmaking
Of a period style that was a little smug—achieved,
And an achievement, but also arch and cold. It didn't take the
Debauchees of Dostoyevsky or *a brokenness perversely*

Planned to be unmanned by memories of pigeon and/or
This girl or that, just brokenness itself. The kind that
Comes quite naturally when one's enamored, still.

Put on someone else's body, then? Breathe with someone
Else's diaphragm and lungs? It can't be done. It can't
Quite be done. Nor can one make love to someone else's
Proud Cyrillic word, breath on its way to a becoming fire,
Imagining a body in transcendent ecstasy. Not quite.
One could not command. But words commanding one instead?
Like *lust?* Like *lust* and *love* comingled and confused. Like
A wholly efficacious speaking out in foreign tongues.

Like Pasternak in speaking out of *Hamlet.* And Doctor Z
Writing in the night while Larissa, Lara, Magdalene sleep on:
I'll play the part, but this time as an unscripted actor. Improv only
As he Hamlets through it all while wind and the wolves howl
And howl and howl? Such an unprotected house for love where
Stepps annihilate most everything that breathes. A thousand sets
Of opera glasses focus from the future as a Russian turns up
Inside out, hand offered, saying *things that you cannot command.*

In a different English than before. *Father,* it says . . . *this cup* . . .
A draught of filiation. *Sackcloth latticed through with
Poignant, italic tremors.* All italics tremble as in some kind
Of primal fear. The God of details is a sexual spark that's lent

From another dynasty to dress the caryatids of infirmity.
One step at a time. One steppe at a time. Whether in Archangel
Or in Denmark or in England. In Poland, Miłosz praised him
Who confronted arguments only with his sacred Slavic dance.

In English it's a fine choreography for someone's *pas de deux*
With Sister Life. Dizzying and dancey, but quite beyond the
Privilege of a body's full embrace. The world's body and
The Word's. Incised as a kind of alphabetic incest, Lot must
Cast his lot in some apocrypha. Love's not a daughter but a
Sister now, the biblical a game of baffle's bluff. Breathing turns
Into a heavy huff and puff. Dissent's dead reckoning. It is.
It is a world fully abdicated, a world full, without contention.

MODERNATO PIZZICATO

O Lynx keep watch on my fire he had written in Pisa
and *Dryad* he'd called her a long time back
and she thought the *new subtlety of eyes* was probably hers
dove sta memoria when she read it in his prison poems
in her Künsnacht sanatorium . . .

E.P. loves H.D.—it could
have been encircled with a heart, carved by a couple of kids
on a tree. From the wreckage of Europe they groped their way
toward what they remembered and loved.
And at Künsnacht that clinic was fine for filming
a bust: Dick and Nicole at Dr. Brunner's healing-place,
Scott loves Zelda carved by actors on the widest conifer.
Pound had put a eucalyptus seed in his coat when
the Partisans marched him away from hills above Rapallo.
It had the face of a cat: *O Lynx keep watch on my fire.*
And she was herself a feline, an eidolon Helen to boot.
As Freud's analysand she watched the local extras in halls,
a rich girl taking the talking cure talking and talking. Change
the movie to *Borderline* and she is the star, a demi-monde
neurotic with her dipsomaniac beau. Who knows why
they're here? Or Jason Robards and Jennifer Jones who
drive each other's Dick & Nic around town; Jill St. John
is no *San Juan with a belly ache writing ad posternos,*

but she squeaks like a ditsy mouse and shows her pointy tits.

What all fits this case? A pretty face, of course,
a march to the line, a dance to the rhythm, the time.
Rhyme it with mime and bring in the rest of the cast:
Tom and Viv, Gertrude and Alice, Nora and Jim—
Billyam Williams and Freytag-Loringhaven the mad.
Ulysses loves Penelope they carve on yet another tree.
Helen's at the door of Dr. Brunner; Paris is a patent fiction
she complains. Let's to Lake Geneva for a sail. P. Pudovkin
writes in *Close-up*, Bryer's cinema mag, regarding the art
of the cut, but who has the knife any more or the nail?
It's closing time at the jail, the privileged asylum,
contagious hospital, letterpress printer's, the ruined town.
Close up the closet of cut-up text & cut out hearts & heroes
cut down to size. Some guy on TV is singing pizzicato lies.
Someone's baby sits right down and cries.

THEIR FLIMS

                   films, that is. A typo just as easy
an essai as William Faulkner's standing
on the set with Howard Hawkes
charged with coming up with something quick to
spice the dialogue in Hem his rival's
Have or Have Not, moved from Florida and Cuba
all the way to Martinique, Hawkes saying
Well well well well   try something
here. And the novelist's response: *Was you*
ever bitten by a dead bee? All for Walter Brennen,
Bogart and Becall gone off already for
a drink with Scott who'd not have bothered with the big
film of 1939 (because by then *The Last*
Tycoon was on the fire) if he hadn't had a contract still
to honor even if he was fifteenth and not the first
to have a go at Miss Leigh's Miss Scarlett.
Their films. Their fame consists of something else,
a flame and flame-out, both. How to have
both haven for a talent in your palm and payment
in your fist to gobsmack anyone who'd
make you write in anagrams derived from text by
Margaret Mitchell? Not a bloody word
you haven't picked with tiny forceps out of Tara's
Torah, mate: When you're bitten by

a dead bee you'll know the nature of a sting-
ing cut, an improvisation by the broad: *You know
how to whistle, don't you?* What's the difference
between Vichy cops and Southern gents
or officers in Rebel uniforms wrapped
like mummies in the Stars and Bars? Bogy's luck
with Miss Becall and Gable's reassurances
that he was never gay didn't trouble pages adding up
in *Absalom* or point of view adjusted in
the fictive life of Irving Thalburg, movie mogul, when
the daughter saying I, I, I has got beyond her depth
and can't produce *Producer's Daughter* as a
college girl at Bennington. What added up was
adding up: the debts. To whom however ask the
question: *Now I owe you one?* The actress on her knees
in some lost outtake in the pre-coded days in Hollywood
saying *Bet you don't believe I ever read your book?*

THE BARONESSES

It's a pity that William Carlos Williams couldn't have met
The Baroness friend of Thelonious Monk instead of
His own Baroness Elsa von Freytag-Loringhoven. No doubt
About it, Baroness Pannonica de Koenigswarter would have
Been a better bet. Although she dug jazz rather than poetry,
Williams would surely have warmed her heart with
His poems about pure products of America, metric figures,
The gold 5 on a fire-truck, lonely streets. He could have
Read them to her in that room with the terrific outlook over
The Hudson where a baby grand and a night of coffee and
Good conversation were always ready for Monk & his friends.
But alas he instead had for his medium longsuffering self
The unwanted attentions of Elsa von Freytag-Loringhoven, a
Baroness Thelonious Monk might have liked. She was
No rich patron, exactly—in fact not at all. Down and out as a
Pure product of America, she might have cadged a drink from
The Baroness Pannonica de Koenigswarter, or just a dime.
Or she might have asked to spend the night in her flat
Or Weehawken house. Lots of people did—and listened to
Records of Horace Silver's "Nica's Dream," Gigi Gryce's
"Nica's Tempo," Kenny Dorham's "Tonica," and of course
The tune by Thelonious Monk, all composed for the former
K.A.P. (for Pannonica) Rothschild who married the pilot
And banker Jules de Koenigswarter (later Minister Plenipo-

Tentiary from France) who himself became embarrassed enough
By her night life to leave her forever when Charlie Parker
Died on her sofa and her "good name" got in the tabloid press.
But in fact they never met, mostly because the poor and crazy
Baroness Elsa von Freytag-Loringhoven died in the gas
That she or her lover allowed to escape in her dingy dada digs
In Rue Barrault on 14 December of 1927, a year when the
Barroness Pannonica de Koenigswarter was still only a girl
Of twelve out in the fields with her gifted father Nathaniel
Charles Rothschild hunting bugs for his entomological pastime
Which etymologically led, said Monk, to her name: Pan-
Nonica of Eastern Europe's Pannonian plain, a butterfly her
Father had found and liked. As for Elsa von Freytag-Loringhoven,
She was hot not for Monk—who after all was only six at the time—
But for William Williams, doctor and poet, thirty-eight in 1921.
She wore a coal-scuttle as a hat, tin cans on her breasts, and
Exhibited with Man Ray and Duchamp in circa those days
A plumbing-pipe she called "God." Williams followed her
Home from the show where she offered to give him
The very thing that he, as a doctor, treated for free in half
His artist friends in New York—a case of the clap.
He withdrew, but she followed. All the way to Williams' house
In New Jersey. At that point everything's right out of
Somebody's travesty of Restoration excess on a Provincetown
Stage: she arrives, he runs, she pursues, he calls for help from
His wife, she curses in German, he shoves her away, she punches

His face, he punches her face, she hides in a tree, he shakes on
Her branch, she falls and stumbling recovers, his wife throws a
Rolling pin in the air, she laughs, he cries, she disappears in the night
With police in hot pursuit and Mrs. W.W. singing out something
A bit like "Well, you needn't" or "By-ya," "Off minor,"
Or "Nutty"—all tunes by Theolnious Monk. Round about midnight
Monk would arrive at Baroness Pannonica's place. There he would
Play the piano for hours, for days. Mostly he didn't talk.
Sometimes he sat and stared at the keys. In the end the Baroness
Took on the jobs that Monk's exhausted wife no longer performed.
She got him to eat, got him to take his pills, got him now and then
Out of the house to perform. She must have loved the man.
He fell at last into a silence deep as Ezra Pound's in Venice.
He no longer played. She let him behave as he liked, dressing up
In his natty way in the morning but lying all day in bed in his
Crisp clean shirt with a coat and tie. That went on for three years.
If Baroness Elsa von Freytag-Loringhoven and William Williams
Had come for a visit or house-call, they would have learned
A thing or two about the pure products of America and respect
Verging on awe. It would have been quiet there as the grave
And tending to the sublime. With Baronesses keeping guard on
Either side of the bed, the doctor poet might have picked the
wet hair from the pianist's eyes and watched him with compassion.

ASHEVILLE OUT

i.m. Charles Olson and Thomas Wolfe

                      so you've only a museum now
and not a college at all
although I understand the buildings still exist near the town
where religion has reclaimed the real estate that
John Rice took for the muses after he scandaled at Rollins
lecturing on the classics in his jock. *What . . . ?* she says—
but she's in Asheville here at the *Mountain Museum*
with Annie Albers and Ruth Asawa and M.C. Richards
Women of the College up on walls
their paintings and prints and stills from documentary films
works and days from the place
where poets, if not painters, were so macho they hadn't the time
to read, for example, Hilda Morley's delicate poems.
Who . . . ? she says, young and pretty docent, and I think
of docile women among genital toughs out there
but also of dear Hilda when I met her, Yaddo in the '70s, when
still she was unpublished, getting really old, still telling
all those stories about Stefan Wolpe's Parkinson's—
little paper-wads of poems slipped under my door at night,
her Dickinsonian habit of abasement followed by abrupt display
of weirdly offered & prodigious genius—
Wolpe her great lover and her husband and the reason why

she didn't publish for so long.
I think the most erotic photograph I've ever seen
was of Hilda once in *Ironwood* where the young and lovely girl
bites into an apple smiling with her eyes at Wolpe
middle-aged and briefly eminent composer
while he grins longing back at her on the Lee Hall front porch
and the grand love between them
positively shimmers in the air, in the lake behind them,
in the green mountains above—

                              and Tom Wolfe only
wanted out
of all this, the hills, the little town, the boarding house
managed by his mum: *Just off the car line;*
Large Lawns, Reasonable Rates, Newly Furnished Throughout.
Our Auto Rides You from the Station for Free
No Sick Folks Here. Did I know, she asks,
any of the really *famous* poets? Dorn, yes; Creeley, yes;
Robert Duncan, yes & for a while & in a way.
'Twas as if I said I'd seen Shelley plain.
Days of *Idaho Out.* Days of *Gloucester Out.* Asheville out beyond and
south I used to drive on family holidays
my father stuck it in reverse on mountain curves because
our Plymouth—1948—couldn't manage the climb
except by backing up. Scott Fitzgerald didn't meet Tom Wolfe
in 1936 because the six-foot-seven native was

in Germany for the Olympics in a U.S. diplomatic box just west
of Hitler on the day that Owens won his first gold.
He exploded in a raucous Rebel cheer that drew the Führer's ire:
Who's the big oaf with their ambassador?
And who's the man in Asheville with the crazy wife
whose books were all the rage before the crash and all
the unemployed, for who cared in 1936 about those flappers
in East Egg or was it West those rich idlers on the Riviera?
I don't know, she says, *but . . .*
nor did the two giants ever meet—had you
asked Wolfe to climb on Olson's shoulders they'd have
been together something getting onto fourteen feet tall
and a useful human ladder for a second-story man breaking
into Biltmore place. But what's the first story
and she says *Did you teach out there yourself?* Of course
Maximus & Eugene Gant never walked along the Blue Ridge Highway
but they might have done it just as my father
might have gotten round that turn and backed the car
to Cherokee where nothing much is going on
beyond the poverty, casino gambling, Indians playing Indians
for some snotty gringo's snotty children now. But then
there was the first story. It's about three bears.
Alas it's true that some men forgot their obligations and
their clan's rites and found themselves with long hair on their bodies
and without their thumbs
and on their hands and knees, the kinsmen still of Hanging Maw

and Double Head and even John Ridge
they assumed names like Jackson Johnson Jefferson
and knew they must be hunted as they hid
until they had to hunt themselves. What kind of creatures
walk together on the road from Asheland out
of caves and down from trees and into talking leaves
inscribed in signs for eighty-six sounds
borrowed by Sequoia from the Greek and Roman and Cyrillic?
What? She says. Days of *Gloucester Out,* I say.
Days of what? she says. Those, I say, were the days.

LONGS AND SHORTS

(for Roy Fisher at eighty)

And will a photograph save us? We're old enough
To have had a temptation to think
That the old cliché about *ars longa* had some
Actual merit. What's long
Are the drifting sands as we plod to the
Music of *vita brevis*. But it *is* a music, tra-la.
It seems but a moment ago you were only 70
And we urged you in your words to
Put the piano at risk, to left-hand us a poem.
But photography's the democratic art.
I just saw a snap of you in South Bend, Indiana
The very night of your reading in 1980.
It was also the first night you'd spent outside
Of Britain: Not in Paris, not in Rome, but
South Bend, Indiana. I can't even say it's the
Midwestern Birmingham, although you
Liked and found familiar the "abandoned workings,"
As W. H. Auden would say, of the old
Studebaker auto plant. After the reading we
Travelled out to the house of a prof
In the same car with another guest of the school
Who seemed even more laid back

Than you, though also a bit incongruous.
He too both wrote and put the piano at risk. He too
Had a cosmopolitan soul. At the party
You sat together on a sofa—clearly someone
Would play. As you jazzed the *vita brevis*
Out of the upright, *Ars Longa* himself
Appeared with his camera. And here in
A short book is the picture long after the music
Has fled. I can see it's my friend Roy Fisher
Fishing for the right notes in a riff.
But the caption grasping at by god immortal life
Declaims like Caesar's newsboy: *John Cage*
Plays four minutes of silence
While on the opposite page Harold Brodkey's
Mislabeled *Joseph Brodsky.*
Irreversible, Roy. But what the hell?

HOMAGE TO G. P-P.:
SMULTRONSTÄLLET

 . . . and someone saying, *Yes
but Göran doesn't really speak good Swedish.*
I looked up, perplexed.
Skanian, he declared. *He's from the south,*
as all of us—Doctor Isak Borg and Marianne,
Sarah, Anders, and Viktor;
Susan, John, and G. Printz-Påhlson—
headed down to Malmö and to Lund.
Smultron's not the same as jordgubbe said
a man in dark glasses sitting right behind us in
the Lane Arts Cinema, Columbus, 1959:
a handless clock, a coffin falling from the hearse,
and top-hatted ancients walking to their
jubeldoktor honors, Borg having dreamed
his way from Stockholm, Sarah both his lost love
and late Fifties girl, just like my Susan, flirting
with the guys in the back seat, chewing on her pipe.
What did I know then of time, of memory, of age?
And who would watch a movie wearing heavy shades?
We looked behind us and he nodded in a formal way.
Göran, ten years my senior, was writing poems
in Malmö that von Sydow liked to read—*Max,*
as he called him, who spoke his Swedish very well

whether as a knight in *The Seventh Seal*
or there before us pumping gas in *Smultronstället*
or when reading Göran's poems to a little
group of connoisseurs. But Max doesn't
get it when the doctor says, mostly to himself,
Perhaps I should have stayed.
We didn't get it either, though we stayed—right
through the film, and trying very hard.
In twenty years I'd introduce my friend from Skania
to my Midwest as Dr. Printz-Påhlson, poet.
A colleague thought that Göran was a royal and
called him *Prince*. Oh, and Göran hated
Bergman films, all that religious angst, which
everybody asked about, even though his lecture was
on Strindberg. So much for the '80s.
In 1959 Bibi Anderson was twenty-two, only
three years older than my girlfriend.
I thought how much I'd like to sleep with her.
The man in sunglasses put his head between us
and said, <u>*Place*</u> *of wild strawberries;*
the English doesn't get it. The car drove on.
Years after Göran got his own degree at Lund, his head
literally belaurelled, little girls in white
throwing flower petals in his path,
he fell all humpty-dumpty down a flight of stairs
and broke his crown on the cement, and lost

his sight, and pushed aside his work, and rests
in silence in a Malmö nursing home. With whom
share a joke, a plate of herrings, bog myrtle schnapps?
The nightmare examiner had said:
You are guilty of guilt
when Isak Borg misdiagnosed his patient, saying
She is dead. You are incompetent, concluded the
examiner, and all of us got back into the car
and headed south: Borg & Marianne; Sarah, Anders, Victor;
Susan, John & Göran; and the man in heavy shades.
The summer sun is blinding, even in the night.
Smultronstället. Wherever we were from,
we couldn't stay.

ANOTHER MOVIE, COLONEL B

Remembering Ian Watt

What they whistled wasn't Malcolm Arnold, 1957,
But Kenneth Alford, 1914. And yet that year after Suez,
Arnold sued a record company for marketing
A march in which the whistle morphed into his own
Counterpointed composition, flutes and drums
And horns celebrating fiction as the facts dropped away
And 1942 sweat out its guts in Technicolor
On a bridge across the wrong bloody river. Just ask
Your professor who had built the real thing and
Told you after twenty years that Jósef Korzeniowski,
Sailor, wasn't an Imperialist. He also told you
He himself awakened once thinking about Conrad's grave
In Dover—why no mention of his wife? Strange
That a starving POW in Thailand would be worried
About that. Might as well go out and watch a movie; might
As well go whistle in descending minor thirds. Bogey did
Exactly that instead of shouting *Fore* when he hooked
His drive. The hidden bird up so high outside my window
That I can't see him now for all the leaves and sun isn't
Shouting *Fore*. He too likes to whistle in descending thirds.
Ti-Dee, Ti-Dee, he sings. *Hi-ro. Hi-to.* His news is
Out of date for heaven's sake. It's 2007 but these musics

Stir a counterpointed theme. I squeeze a girl's hand as a
Train chugs through the jungle toward the cantilevered artifact
An English Colonel loves, sabotaged by other Brits.
Six years later and I'm in the Stanford office of my teacher
Talking fiction. What are facts? What are railway tracks
Running all the way from Bangkok to Rangoon?
The real thing. The hammering of iron spikes rang with a
Reason for the working party on a slick embankment.
He could hear it still. What I heard along with what he said
Was Malcolm Arnold's take on Alford's Limey tune; what
I saw was lifted up by hired Danish engineers in Thai
Ceylon across a stretch of river unremarked on any map.
They'd mastered the resistance figures and the coefficients,
Knew the depths to which the piles needed to be sunk.
When the bridge is finished there is cabaret, applause—
A celebration where the weary Brits congratulate
Themselves at complicated intervals: 14, 42, 57, 63—
Multiply them each by each and find their roots.
The boots of all the men who worked had rotted off their feet.
The river valley was as dark as an entire continent in
Joseph Conrad's heart. What did Ian Watt care about
The grave of Jessie C in Dover as he starved in Thailand,
Talked to me in 1963? What? I kissed the girl and missed
The great explosion, bridge and train plunging in a Khai
They'd found for movie moguls threading through
a lush jungle in which William Holden, Yank who

Outmaneuvers Alec Guinness at his game, escapes. Jessie C
Wanted an elaborate marble monument outlasting all
The sales of her husband's books; hence her
Name was missing on Korzeniowski's simple stone.
Colonel Bogey only wanted not
To hook his drive; Malcolm Arnold wanted credit for his march
Derived from Alford's take on Bogey's whistle, music
Worth an Oscar and the royalties from
Hyperdrive, *The Breakfast Club*, and MasterCard
Whose adverts started off in minor thirds like
Claims for territory made above me by the hidden bird.
On your Internet connection you can book
A 13:20 train from Bangkok which will cross the right river
On the wrong bridge in the least time. Just past Kanchanburi.
The man who'd write a book about the book I'd read
The night before in 1963 had wanted to survive forced labor
Still alive and write it. He nearly died. He wanted
In a long digression just to make me see the travesty of
Honor, work and order represented by the monument a
Fictive English officer had caused to be
And toward which all the singing and the whistling rose.
My own hand I wanted on my pretty girl's breast.
So what's the test? Blacklisted writers had their names
Erased from screens while on the scrim of history
A script was beamed for ministers & patrons, dignitaries—
Wives and pretty daughters wearing Ascot hats—

Who'd come out from the capital to see the blast . . .
Which capital? The last before the failed coup or latest
Occupation anywhere, Bogey's whistlers listing for a hunt,
A hint of fame, a name put up in lights. The nights in fact
Brought nothing but despair and total dark, Conradian.
The last shot's the bridge in ruins taken from
A helicopter rising in the sky like music or a poet's lark
And flying on toward Vietnam. Mistah Watt—he was
Annoyed by that, whose bandog-days hadn't lost their bark.

ASSOCIATIONAL POEM FOR PETER ROBINSON AT SIXTY

The great cellist, Pablo Casals, was asked on
His ninetieth birthday why he continued to
Practice for five hours every day. He said:
"I'm making progress." I just saw a picture
Of you on Facebook—playing guitar in a
Rock group! I trust you're making progress.
When I was thirty-five or so and you
A decade younger, we both lived on what you
Called Inertial Road in Cambridge. Our first
Conversations were in your attic flat.
Herschel Rd. still looks much the same, but
You and I do not. I'm headed fast for
The geezer class, but hope I'm making progress
Even now at writing poems. When you
Put down your guitar, that's what you do too.
At least when you're not painting watercolours
Like "The Clothes Chair" and the unfinished
Painting of Yagiyama, Sendai, on the cover of
The Look of Goodbye. You flipped me a look of
Goodbye when you departed South Bend, Indiana
After having read from your translations of
Vittorio Sereni at my university. With Italian,
You've always made great progress, though

I wonder if your Japanese isn't getting rusty
Now that you're living back in Britain, having
Overcome inertia well beyond its Cambridge road
By making progress in Sendai and Italy.

Coming to South Bend, you were drafting something
Later called "Enigma Variations," the title meant
To reference not just Elgar but De Chirico, whose
Doppelgänger stood up at your reading in Chicago
And volunteered a question. What did he ask?
Your poem doesn't say. Maybe something enigmatic
Like, "Did you find the poets in Japan a bit Italian,
Or would you say more British or American?"
Clutching your bilingual U of C edition of Sereni,
You caught The South Shore train, writing on the way
Perhaps the only poem in English about stations
On that route from Randolph Street to Gary Metro,
Hudson Lake, and points beyond. The run-down
Neighborhoods along the way must have looked familiar
To a Brit from Leeds (born not far from where McCartney
Met John Lennon), just the way, as you'll remember,
The ruined workings of the South Bend Studebaker plant
Looked familiar to our friend Roy Fisher
Fresh from Birmingham. . .

            . . . Had you stayed in town

For more than just a day, we might have made you
Honorary laureate of the Midwestern rustbelt, but
You had to leave for Parma and Giuseppe Verdi Airport.
At Michiana Regional the airlines didn't substitute for
Elevator music arias from *Traviata* or *Otello* (even
With TB and murder on the rise, Vittorio Sereni Englished
In your bag). Waiting for your flight you wrote the
Section of "Enigma Variations" on departure. Have you
Ever noticed that *Enigma* almost anagrams *Imagine?*
What's added on is an extra I. I've always liked the
Fine eye in your poems, and for that matter also
The reticent (and English) "I." I hope your subtle ear
Isn't damaged by this recent flirting with the
Rock and roll, but no one knows these days when
A Facebook photo is a meme, and that's my only
Evidence of this indulgence, granted to us all, in one
Form or another, once we're over sixty. (Anyway, all
Poetry began as song.) Like Casals at ninety,
I hope we both keep making progress—when in Rome
Or Reading, Sandai or South Bend. But even if
We do, we know life's an enigma. And so, imagine.

ROMULUS AT YADDO

Did you have nicknames? Judy asked,
And you said *Only as a boy—Rom, Rommy*
You supposed, were more or less required.
But now I'm only Romulus, and I thought
Only in what sense? Only that and wishing
It were more? Or, And it's a good thing, too.

We'd sit around your tower room in that
Big house. "Residents" all, we had unequal
Grants—some for a month, some for the
Summer, some that seemed forever. There were
Tales of people who just never left, people
Who had died there ghosting now in hallways

Late at night, making jokes out of mortality
Like you when joking in your *Jesus Tales,*
Your forgotten book, but one I loved in part because
I heard it all from you as with your actor's voices
You played every part for just an audience of two:
Judith Moffett and myself.

Christ walked your hillbilly mountains with his
Pal called Pete to make his story clear to
The illiterate. First he had to make them laugh.

A joshing Jesus. A joshing Simon Peter too.
A letter falls from the book that's dated 1981.
I'm anxious that your people there not think

It sacrilegious or satirical or anti-Christian.
After all our laughter in the summer, you were
Going to read from *Jesus Tales* at Notre Dame
Once the book was printed. Two nuns left
The auditorium. A lay-brother booed. And you?
You hyperventilated on the stage and had

To catch your breath, pause for a sip
Of moonshine. Afterwards, we talked about
Our Lauras, your daughter and my own. I asked you
Which Linney lines would last. You said
The Laura lines. I couldn't have agreed any more.
Always straight man with my brilliant friends,
I said: *Your Jesus joke is Logos for the Gens!*

WALTER'S HOUSE: HOMAGE
TO WALT DAVIS

[while passing on the Campion to Cornelius Eady]

I know it's Walter's house no longer,
But I think of it, because I've thought of it
That way for thirty years and more,
As Davis Place. For far too long it was
Entirely empty. When I was young and just
Had come to town, he welcomed me,
Passing on *The Works of Thomas Campion*
He'd edited that very year, 1967.
It was the year I married. It was a year
When one could still persuade oneself
That the Sixties, whose veterans now are sixty,
Might in fact still usher in Aquarius by way
Of a machinery concealed by some Inigo
Within the fantasy of its extraordinary masque
Performed in Caesar's court . . .

          From our house to yours,
The inscription reads, *with hopes*
For every kind of harmony forever. I'd sit there
In his study imitating gruff Yvor Winters
Gruffly reading *Now Winter Nights*, and claim

That I had Stanford friends—Pinsky,
Hass and Peck—who had written poems already
That would matter. He drank too much,
Like Winters, and he told me in his cups
The price he'd paid for scholarship, the expense
Of spirit and the loss of years in dusty rooms
And half-lit archives. But his study was ablaze
With light and insight.

                    When winter nights enlarged
The number of their hours, I'd walk South Bend's
Park Avenue and wish it were New York's.
Sometimes very late, one or two a.m., I'd pass his house
And see the beam across the snow from where his
Curtains didn't meet. He was still up and working.
First at his desk, then at the harpsichord, the Gamba,
Picking out an aire, testing theory against meter against
Song—*Goe, numbers, boldly pass*—with speaking voice
And then with instruments . . . In 1600 there went forth
From Campion a treatise where, he said,
It was "demonstratively proved" that
Quantitative counting was not cant in English.
Walter loved the massed sounds of strophes all full
Of l's and e's and o's, or lines all keyed to single
Vowel: *O then I'le shine forth as an Angell of light.*
He played through scales in tetra chords, listened

For the semitones, and anchored counterpointing
With the bass. *Nympha potens Thamesis*
Soli cessura Dianae raised her head above the ice
Of Campion's Latin verse. The Thames
Was the St. Joseph River, and the lady listened with me
In the night. She counted quantities
But looked like Bessie Smith. We thought we heard

A new music in that house that for so long
Was still. A poet filling up the walls again with books,
The study as a student of the word & song.
Among the maskers linger ghostly Lords like Scrope & North,
But Counts like Basie, Dukes like Ellington, emerge.
The innovative chords are Monk's.
When we walk along the street at night
We think we hear the lute of Muddy Waters
And Chicago Blues . . .

       Cornelius, I thought I'd
Pass on Thomas Campion because he lived so long in
Walter's mind who lived so long where you've arrived,
Bringing with you poetries to make a madrigal
Of time and circumstance, contingencies
And synchronicity. Take what you've said—*a motion,*
Gambling's pitch, holding back and laying out,
Slow-mo chop-time logic lifted up & then away that

You can sing. Invite Walt Davis to the house warming
With his book of ayres, his sackbuts and his
Gambas and his viols . . . And then shine forth.
Then shine forth like Angels.

O then shine forth like Angels of the light.

VI

DES PETITS HOMMAGES

MALLARMÉ

No tomb here for Edgar Poe or Baudelaire or Anatole

(Nor
For Couperin, my most revered Ravel)

\#

Debussy winds up Baryshnikov as Balanchine observes
from the wings

his faun

one Sunday afternoon at Saratoga springs

bullet/hashtag/dingbat

*

It's the dancer's debut with the NYC Ballet and the
audience has come
some distance just to see him jump
although he only hugs the earth
and snake-like
writhes

126

(a little joke by the choreographer but not
On Mallarmé
whose poem keeps saying what it said
To begin with
Si clair leur incarnat léger   qu'il voltige dans l'air

The dance, the music, is only a "Prelude
to *L'Après-Midi*
d'un faune"
and the nymphs he sees and would perpetuate.
Which must mean that it's morning.
Whatever else could a prelude to an afternoon be?
And postlude, please, for an evening

(by which time it very likely will be mourning)
Assoupi de sommeils touffus.

BURGOYNE AND GATES

Neither one of them anticipated Mallarmé
But Saratoga was a dance
That brought the French into the war, official favor
More than just
The presence of the young Lafayette

#

Nor did their dance prefigure Debussy
Baryshnikov & Balachine.
But Mallarmé and Debussy might well have drawn
The doubledance in sometime's re-
enactment more inspired by
Josh Reynolds and Gilbert Stuart portraits than by
hurling in the battle of the

Bullets/hashtags/dingbats

Neither general got a new command

@

what cost the arts of war?

strategy admits its own strange gratuity

it's beautiful then?

From a distance
From a distance that is very great

RIMBAUD/RAINBOW/SVENBRO

Jesper Svenbro's Noah's Ark gets stuck on
Big Mount Aigert
Because, he says, of faulty navigation.

Never mind

The mountain animals all tumble out: lemming & lynx
Bear, squirrel, fox, otter, moose
And wolverine

Also the hare, whose job is to lift a prayer
To the rainbow, which word,
Because of a speech impediment, he is unable
To pronounce

And so
Calls out as the morning sun shines down on the
Dara headland:

RIMBAUD

Who in fact appears, and is described in
Svenbrovian apochrapha
As he walks down the mountain dressed in a blue coat

Common among Laps who lived and fished
In those parts a century ago

#

He was headed "northward"—*Norwege*—that's to say
Toward Norway in the etymological sense
With his kit for an Orpheus Poem

ORPHEUS

emerges from the kit that Rimbaud carries down the mountain.
The kit makes O. "faithful to a poetics
Of the lumber-language poem,"
but kit-bearer R. leaves him to his own devices to catch
a fast train to Stockholm. He's been
elected to that committee that gives out noble *pis*
(pronounce that *pies*: as in apple, cherry, etc.
Or multiply by 3.14159)

Orpheus, an Oldforest Pine, escaped the fire
as well as the flood when
he disassembled himself in the kit.
Now he strides ahead.
Apollo *Terbintheus*, the turpentine god,
the pine forest god, allows him to play the woods
out of the underworld.

For these fine thoughts Rimbaud/Rainbow argues
that Jesper Svenbro, maker of
the kit that contained the actual Orpheus
all through the period of the flood
should win a *pi,* the very *pi,* in fact,
that he badly wants for himself.

Re-enters the stammering hare

r,r,r,r, RAINBOW he says
and Rimbaud rises into the sky with his arms
outstretched
and looking confused.

Oldforest Orpheus grows moss, lichen,
grows tall, grows old, grows
a green head full of birds and little forest creatures
not afraid of heights.

Svenbro in his Orpheus poem makes a little river run
where he drowns the kit
with the spawning chars and wading fisher-folk.

LYDIA DAVIS

Among the titles of her works my favorite is
"Meat, My Husband"
But when it comes to Marcel Proust her translation of
The first book is the traditional: *Swann's Way*.
It might have been "The way by Swann's" in order to avoid
Ambiguity.
Swann's way of doing things isn't really recommended.
Before Odette became his wife
And was still a lady of the night as well as his
Particular mistress, would he
Have introduced her (in French of course an entire
New sequence of double entendres
Would be needed): "Meat, My Future Wife."

\#

Is translation *Un Coup De Des*?
"Even when launched in eternal circumstances
From the depths of a shipwreck?"
(*Le Viande, Mon Mari* doesn't do the job at all)

JAMAIS

Proust for Pleasure / Mallarmé for Pain
A misprint of course for *pain*
For bread: Mallarmé for daily bread, *le pain*.
Or a misprint for Pan?
The very afternoon of which the Goatlike God is
Celebrated in the poem
Whose prelude played such pretty pipes
In pentatonic
For the Roman version *faunus*.

FAUN / FAUNE

Mon Dieu, Merci: Por le viande et le pan et le vin

ANTHONY BURGESS

Wrote on the spot a bassoon sonata for my friend
Alison while also explaining over dinner
The lecture he was about to give on "The Devil's Mode."

The Tritone, that is.
He also told a story in which Claude Debussy finds
And is converted to it playing
on an out of tune piano in a house of ill repute.

He'd set the Eiffel Tower to music if
It paid him more
than the *Chat Noir* by the hour.
For Alison, Anthony, like Claude, was Devilish:
Be, he said, like
Old church crooners and carousers of the monody. Be the
Alto who cannot reach
The treble notes.
Ill augment 4 or see you flatten 5

"A fourth lower, Dear, on your bassoon"

1889

and it was Erik Satie who really climbed the Eiffel Tower
Fourths on top of fourths.
Modus diaobli! Claude and that commission he
Could not fulfill to set a mad poem by Mallarmé,
But perhaps just a Prelude?

(Summer in the '70s)

& music fills the body of Baryshnikov at Saratoga just
As it did my friend's Bassoon.
Just
As the bodies of Burgoyne and Gates
Filled the canvases of their proud respective portraits
Just
As lead filled the bodies
Of the battle's fallen.
Does chromaticism win the day?
A whore's piano? The *si fa* condemned once by the church?

GUY DAVENPORT

You'd meet him at strange places
Where every force evolves a form, where geography shapes
The imagination
Or following the Hunter Gracchus with a backpack
Full of Greek poems, *The Anathemata*
Of David Jones, Zukofsky's bewilderments, Spinoza's tulips
And maybe the plans for
Tatlin's tower.

#

Satie would only climb the Eiffel in his forths
But Guy could climb
Tatlin even though it was never built

#

Was he a pornographer?
There are pictures and passages of prose that come close to that
But mainly he was a celebrant.
Letters from him were a joy, always with a Greek salutation.
Phone calls? Who else would talk to you
For two hours about G.M. Doughty's
Arabia Deserta, doing you the honor to suppose you'd read it.

&

he'd have liked the Burgess piece on the augmented fourth
and could play the tritone in his mind
like a triangle. When asked by a journalist about his impeccable
scholarship, he said: "I just like learning things."
You'd have thought he might choose Paris, Rome, or Crete for
His domicile, but he stayed in Kentucky.
What lucky students he had!

In an astonishingly simple poem, he looked across the river
At my home state

France is my watchlight   Ireland's my strong arm,
Grow me a pear tree,
England is my tree,   Germany's my word,
a daughter of the sun.
Spain is my city wall,   Ohio my heart's love
Put yellow pears upon it
My sword is Italy   And prophecy my Lord
And bless them every one.

VII

CÉLESTE, MARCEL, VINTEUIL, AND JUSTICE

CÉLESTE ALBARET, HOUSEKEEPER

I

       Lac Léman, he'd said. And told her that was where
Lord Byron and Madame de Staël had stayed, where
He had first got something right about unconscious memory. He'd
Ended one book there in order to begin the great unfinished one
That she was part of, that everyone he'd known was part of,
That would in the end restore the works of time in place
Of places that at first appeared to wash them all beyond recall like
Ripples from a boat across Geneva's lake . . .

At least that's what she thought he'd said. This man Belmont
Again had asked her to explain what she'd explained
Already. It was, she saw, a kind of test. He'd ask the same question
Several times and watch her closely. Once again she'd answer
As she had before. *Lac Léman*, she said he'd said. *And suddenly*
Sensation of congruence & a joy altogether inexplicable until the ripples
From a boat converge from memory's Beg-Meil & she says Time it's
Time for you to go and he says Sodomite certainly Monsieur

As everyone but you maintains and she says *No I would have known*
Since I knew everything and anyway you've asked me this
A dozen times. She has her tests for him as well. Who is he, after all?
A friend of Henry Miller, the American pornographer. Monsieur
Has now been dead for sixty years. Do the young read Henry Miller in

Translations by Belmont? He uses words Monsieur would never
Want to see in print. Nor would she, a woman over eighty—but not
Without desire. For the truth at least, spoken into a machine.

II

That whirs like Krapp's last tape. Georges Belmont has told her
About Beckett and his play in which an old man speaks into a little
Microphone reciting memories of his past like she does now—Beckett
Yet another one of Belmont's friends who wrote about Monsieur.
He reads to her from *Sodom and Gomorrah* where she's called by her
Own name, a maid in Balbec at the Grand Hotel. She speaks there as
She did of Monsieur as a bird, *pecking his croissant and preening*
Feathers, deep-eyed mischief, raven hair. Has she read the passage?

Has she read the book? Did she say that to him, Belmont asks, or did
He make it up? *How much of his book have you been reading in these*
Sixty years? Another test. She wonders if he'll put words in her
Mouth. She's heard he had another name, was in the Occupation busy
In suspicious ways. It's one thing to be friends with Henry Miller and
Another with the Vichy bureaucrats working with Pétain, Pierre Laval.
Belmont carries on about the Sodomites. He'll be, she understands, her
Voice and vehicle, the presence of her past in some dim future.

She says *he'd have his coffee just exactly so. Night turned to day*
And day to night. Everything was upside down. Time did not have hours,
Only things to do. Like him she was a bird but one that sang and
Hopped from branch to branch. She brought the water bottles made
The fire delivered letters for him cleaned the room if he were out and
Picked up all the towels he dropped. *He awoke at four p.m. and wrote*
All night, eating almost nothing. He shut out all the sun and burned
The powders that would help him breathe. He disconnected phones.

III

Her own phone rings. She picks it up. *No,* she says, *I'm far too busy
And I will be for some time.* But she chats politely for a moment
While Belmont thumbs a copy of *Le Monde* with articles on Watergate,
Although he's thinking about Dreyfus and not Nixon. He's thinking
About loyalty and then he thinks about the very awkward case of
Georges Pelerson. He *is* Georges Pelerson. Celeste hangs up and then
Begins at once where she left off: *Yes, yes the cork lined walls the sealed
Windows fires in summer winter coats. Yes, yes he'd been a Dreyfusard.*

*You know all that. He wouldn't flee the city in the war. He had a special
Kind of courage. I'd go to the basement; he'd go out into the night.* He
Asks her if she still remembers doing Gide, her parody of *Les Nourritures,*
And she says *Oh Nathanaël, I will speak to thee of Monsieur's lady friends.
There is she who made him go out after many years, taxi to the Ritz,
Bell-hops, tips, exhaustion.* And of course Monsieur did go out to the Ritz,
Though not with Gide. Belmont's working nights on *Fear of Flying;*
Suddenly he's got the French for that repeating phrase, *a zippered fuck . . .*

History's a tangle here, but he will sort it all out in the book. *No,* she says,
He never lived in Le Cuziat's male brothel; yes I'm sure Agostinelli
Wasn't Albertine. It's true he went out in the night to watch a flagellation
As research. And other ghastly acts. He'd tell me all about them just
As if he'd been to some soirée at Countess Greffulhe's. All analysis and
Distance, objectivity. *No he didn't drink much alcohol or take those
Drugs you say but just caffeine & powders though he disinfected letters and
Could only look through windows at the hawthorn he had loved.*

IV

Of course she was a prisoner, she knows that. Everyone he knew
Became a prisoner of his book, but there they'll live in time
Beyond their times. Belmont still fears he'll live as Pelerson, who
Swept away his footprints leading to her door. In 1982 Maria Jolas
Will declare that Georges Belmont does not exist, that she and
Joyce and Beckett only knew a Georges Pelerson, collaborationist, who
Calls himself another name & hasn't a remembrance of things past.
In 1982 *Monsieur Proust* will be a German movie called *Céleste*—

Music by Quartet Bartholdy playing César Franck. *No, she says, it's*
Altogether nonsense that Monsieur set out for that quartet to
Play the Franck carrying a large tureen of soup. He did awake them, one
By one, and brought them back at great expense to play for him. He
Needed one more time to hear the little phrase and all its metamorphoses.
(Belmont's now forgotten his solution for *a zippered fuck.*) *Monsieur*
Once found himself at dinner next to Churchill's table at the time of
Peace talks at Versailles. Then I nearly died of Spanish influenza.

But the quartet. He asks once more if that was 1916 and, if there was no
Tureen of soup, didn't she provide some fried potatoes and champagne
When they arrived? She says *he wept the day Jaurés was shot; he hated*
War but loved his country. Franck & France. They played for him the same
Year as Verdun. She doesn't ask *Were you a Nazi?* and he rewinds just
A bit and thinks of Krapp in Beckett saying *spool spoooool—box three &*
Spool five and then of Nixon quoted in *Le Monde* maintaining *No erasures*
On those tapes. She thinks about the index in that book he has, her name.

V

P spends time in conversation with; burns P's notebooks; taking P's
Dictation; pasting manuscripts; parody of Gide; finding spectacles for P . . .
It's like a tape, a movie. Click & whir and flipping over pages in the
Third biography: *Burns his notebooks & There aren't any gaps!* Krapp is
Saying *Face she had! The eyes!* Georges Belmont is saying *Pelerson*
At some tribunal, disappearing for a decade without civil rights but with
The Henry Millers, *Capricorn* for starters, and a new career that's
Brought him, very busy, to her side. He told her *You must trust me!*

She feels like a theme in César Franck's sonata or a train ride to Cabourg—
A transcribed interview, a Google search before its time. For years they've
Sought her out and she has kept her silence. Alone all night he practiced
Death but also resurrection in the word, *déflagration.* Results 1–10
Of some 1,000 for *Céleste Albaret* (0.11 seconds): Poster, News & Forum,
See new play at Steppenwolf . . . *an unlettered girl lived a dream. She was*
The confidante & maid & mother surrogate . . . Or was that *Poster-nude,*
A fettered girl? She doesn't say *And you, were you the Jugendfüher?*

She says again *It's time for you to go.* He will not find the sky outside all
Full of Gothas, Zeppelins, or the biwing Valkyries spiraling in spotlit
Crossbeams up. He's coming down from what for seven weeks has kept
Him high. She doesn't say *I loved him* and he doesn't ask *Did he love you?*
She says *Monsieur liked the Abbé Mugnier who used to say Of course*
We know that Hell exists, but no one's in it. She asks *And all these people*
reading Henry Miller or Miss Jong—why not read Monsieur instead?

He says, *They don't have time.* She smiles . . . And then he's gone . . .

Through her window spring pollens blow & settle over miles & miles.

PROUST IN FIVE PAGES: DONALD JUSTICE'S "LITTLE ELEGY FOR CELLO AND PIANO"

Everybody who reads Proust, along with many people who haven't, knows all about the "little phrase" by the fictional composer Vinteuil which, for Charles Swann, like the madeleine, the sensation of uneven paving stones, and the stiffness of a napkin brought to the lips for the narrator, suddenly opens involuntary memory that comes upon him like a vision of another world. The other world, however, is this world—radiant with past emotion suddenly made present long after an event or experience or place has been left behind by the conscious memory or distorted by intellectual falsifications. After some nine hundred pages, Proust's narrator finally generalizes about this mysterious and unwilled vision to which the reader has been permitted to attain vicarious access.

These bursts of vision triggered by some physical sensation associated with an original experience as it actually transpired, along with the original emotion motivated and felt, are among the reasons we return to Proust. Perhaps the most mysterious among these triggers is the "little phrase" by Vinteuil. By the end of *Swann's Way*, Proust seems even more interested in the five notes by Vinteuil than he is in the relationship between Swann and Odette.

There has been endless speculation about an actual musical source for the sequence of notes that appear in Vinteuil's sonata for piano and violin that becomes the phrase that will evoke Swann's feeling for Odette at various stages of *In Search of Lost Time*.

Was it Saint-Saëns? Debussy? Franck? Fauré? Or perhaps it was the nearly unknown Gabriel Pierné, the candidate put forward by Maria and Natalia Milstein, who also perform his Sonata for violin in D minor, Opus 36, along with music by other contenders, on a recent CD. It doesn't really matter, of course, though Vinteuil's little phrase matters profoundly. Having worked its magic in the early days of Swann's courtship of Odette, it returns at the end of the *Recherche* to contrast what Swann thought he remembered and felt with what the trigger of hearing the "little phrase" long after the relationship had soured actually made manifest for him as a kind of extended epiphany. As Proust writes toward the end of his novel,

> Remembering with what relative indifference
> Swann years ago had been able to speak of the
> days when he had been loved, because what he
> saw beneath the words was not in fact those days

but something else, and on the other hand the
sudden pain which he had been caused by the
little phrase of Vinteuil when it gave him back the
days themselves, just as they were when he had felt
them in the past, I understood clearly that what
the sensation of the uneven paving-stones, the
stiffness of the napkin, the taste of the madeleine
had reawakened in me had no connection with
what I frequently tried to recall to myself . . . .
If, owing to the work of oblivion, the returning
memory can throw no bridge, form no connecting
link between itself and the present minute, if it
remains in the context of its own place and date,
if it keeps its distance, its isolation in the hollow
of a valley or upon the highest peak of a mountain
summit, for this very reason it causes us suddenly
to breath a new air, an air which is new precisely
because we have breathed it in the past, that purer
air which the poets have vainly tried to situate in
paradise and which could induce so profound a
sensation of renewal only if it had been breathed
before, since the true paradises are the paradises
that we have lost.

There, at the end of a very long novel is an expla-
nation of its very *raison d'etre*. But I have written and

quoted at some length really to introduce a very short story that has deep and moving affinities with Proust, Donald Justice's "Little Elegy for Cello and Piano." One might exaggerate the virtues of Justice's restraint by claiming that he gets most of Proust's great theme into six notes discussed in five pages of prose. Or five words in both cases: "The little phrase by Vinteuil"; "The six notes by Bestor."

Eugene Bestor is Justice's composer, and the music that haunts the narrator is Bestor's "Little Elegy for Cello and Piano." The composer's wife and narrator's sister is the cellist who will play with an unnamed pianist in a gallery of the Phillips Collection one December evening in Washington, D.C. Her name is Florence, and she has been married to Eugene "for more than thirty years, and it is clear that they had weathered out whatever storms had come their way"—unlike, we might add, Swann and Odette. Before the performance, the three have tea and cakes at an outdoor café. Someone strolls by "whistling an odd little tune none of us could identify." This is a nice detail given that the music about to be performed will, by the end of the story, have been forgotten by everyone except the narrator.

Before the premier of Bestor's "Little Elegy," there is a piece performed by Fauré during which the narrator's mind drifts and his associations become entangled with Bonnard's painting, *La Grande Terrasse*, which is in the gallery. The narrator is struck by the resemblance of a couple in the painting to Florence and Eugene, "but translated now into a sort of paradise made up all of flowers and light." When Bestor's "Little Elegy" is performed, the narrator thinks of it as "a sort of fantasia in one long movement, and also "a perfect consonance with the Bonnard painting." But at last this short piece— about twelve minutes long we are told—breaks free of all associations, even achieving "an existence apart" from the exact sounds the composer imagined. "They momentarily had a life of their own, beyond us all." At one point, breaking the elegiac solemnity of the elegy, the composer sneezes.

In spite of one "obliterated little passage" caused by the sneeze, the narrator decides that the "Little Elegy" is Bestor's masterpiece, and it is only now that we are given some sense of the composer's background—"the hard early years of study and practice here and abroad, the thousands of mornings of seclusion in his studio, the remarkable ear, the near-photographic memory and recall . . ." and otherwise a rather anonymous life, convention-ally happy in his marriage, but otherwise not unlike Vinteuil's anonymous life as a piano teacher in Proust's Combray. We are to understand that Vinteuil's sonata, like the "Little Elegy," is also a masterpiece, though it will be remembered while Bestor's Elegy will not. Indeed, Vinteuil's success is entirely posthumous.

Justice tells us that Bestor died shortly after the premier of his piece, and that he may have considered it an elegy for himself. His manuscripts have come down to the narrator, who will eventually deposit them in a Vermont college archive. The "Little Elegy" was never performed again. A second performance was scheduled, but Florence became ill and the concert had to be cancelled. Eventually she, too, died, leaving her brother to remember the music which he assumes he is the last living person to hear in his memory a certain phrase—six notes actually reproduced in musical notation—"a little upward rush and subsiding of notes that has come to represent some nameless feeling which otherwise has no voice or expression. It is not exactly that I hear it. It is just there, and I do not of course know what it means."

What the narrator does know, as Justice's story concludes, is that it "had all come down to this, this one ghostly phrase. And soon there will be no one at all to remember how even these six notes sounded."

In *Swann's Way*, Proust writes many pages about Vinteuil's little phrase, about what it means for Swann, and what, we might say, it means in itself. We know what it meant for Swann early on—the little phrase was "their song," his and Odette's, and there is even a time when Swann insisted that Odette play it again and again on the piano while also kissing him. But the little phrase grows in meaning and depth and independence. The more haunted Swann becomes by the phrase the more he begins to think of Vinteuil more than Odette. "And for the first time Swann's thoughts turned with a stab of pity and tenderness to Vinteuil, to that unknown, sublime brother who must also have suffered so; what must his life have been like?"

But, while finally sympathizing with Vinteuil's suffering, Swann sees the little phrase in its own terms, the music uncovered rather than invented by the composer: "The composer had merely unveiled it, made it visible, with his musical instruments . . . . Never had spoken language been such an inflexible necessity, never had it known such pertinent questions, such irrefutable answers." When Swann manages to have a final chance to hear Vinteuil's work, it appears as "made of [a] dais, where a soul had thus been summoned, one of the noblest altars on which a supernatural ceremony could be performed."

Although Proust does not provide, as Justice does, an actual score, his analysis of the little phrase is quite specific. "He had realized that it was to the closeness of the intervals between the five notes that composed it, and to the constant repetition of two of them, that was due this impression of a frigid and withdrawn sweetness." He knew "that in the past he had reasoned in his mind not about the phrase itself, but about simple values substituted for the convenience of his intelligence." But now the "mysterious entity" stands forth to be perceived "as a thing in the world, like some real object." By this point Odette hardly matters at all. "We will perish, but we have for hostages these divine captives who will follow us and share our fate. And death in their company is less bitter, less inglorious, perhaps less probable."

Is this what Donald Justice's narrator feels as he approaches death? We have more of a sense of Bestor's music being left behind with no one to hear it rather than functioning as a "divine captive which will follow us and share our fate." But whether such numinous forms follow us or stay behind, Justice and Proust, when thinking of their particular composer's musical phrase understand, as Swann discovers, that such things "exist latent in the mind in the same way as certain other notions without equivalents, like the notion of light, of sound, of perspective . . . We can no more eliminate our experience of them than we can our experience of some real object, than we can for example doubt the light of the lamp illuminating the metamorphosed objects in our room when even the memory of darkness has vanished."

One could move on from Justice's exquisite short story to his poem on the very same subject called "The Sunset Maker" or his affectionate accounts, in verse and in prose, of his childhood piano teachers. But I'll end this with a quote that appears as a kind of epigraph to *A Donald Justice Reader* identified only as "from the draft of a story." It must have been an alternative ending to "Little Elegy for Cello and Piano." I rather wish he had retained it.

Yet I do not doubt the existence somewhere—in the atmosphere, let us say—of a sort of eternity of sounds. I am told there are scientific grounds to believe this. And in this eternity of sounds Eugene's rich, exact notes persevere. They continue, they repeat themselves, they endure—a form of energy, pure energy of the pure spirit. I cannot hear them, or many of them, but I believe they are there, like the laughter on old radio shows or the conversations of Goethe, like the sword-sounds of dim medieval battles or the dark surf Homer himself heard without seeing.

PROUST AND JUSTICE

His old friend's papers came down to him.
The scores, not too many. He assumes they'll
End in an archive. Does he read music?
A little. He can hum the five notes that he
Remembers from a performance years ago
Of Bestor's "Little Elegy for Cello and Piano."
He wrote a story about it, and that was the title.
It was the title, therefore, of both the composition
And the story written about its performance.
About its only performance. He also wrote a poem
About the same subject called "The Sunset Maker."
In it he says, "And who plays Bestor now?"
That's much like what I imagine Proust's Vinteuil
Thinking to himself at the end: "Who will play
Vinteuil now." When is now? No Bestor now.
No Vinteuil now. No Justice now. The author of
The poem and story is Justice, Donald. But
When is now? One can only guess at the sound
Of Vinteuil's "little phrase." But I have just
Asked a friend to play the six notes of Bestor's
On a piano and send me a sound file. I do not
Find them memorable. And yet in Justice, both
His narrator in the story and his speaker
In the poem remember them. Is that Justice?

Perhaps it's just Donald. The poem quotes
Stravinsky saying that music must be abstract.
That's not, as I remember, in the story. The poem
Says, "I hear it. It is just there. I don't say what
It means." But of course, that doesn't happen now
As I read it, and is long past when I write this
Down now (which now is already past in its turn.)
I asked a friend who worked with Justice, "was
Bestor real?" The answer was "he is now."
There we are again. We could also ask, Is there
Justice in Proust. The answer is yes, in many
Ways, but to keep it simple: Dreyfus was
Exonerated and the Dreyfusards rejoiced. But
That was then. You read about it in histories
Of France. We might also ask, Is Proust in
Justice? I think the answer must be yes given,
In the story, a moment when the four characters
Eat some biscuits and drink tea while someone
Whistles a tune that no one can identify. Isn't
That a little nudge about the madeleine in
Swann's Way and Marcel's involuntary memory
Rushing at him as he dips the fat cookie in
The tea and tastes the past. He tasted the past?
In what was "now" for him, though maybe not
For Proust. Was that Justice? Stravinsky once
Again: Music is abstract. Is Language? To a degree,

But not in quite the same way. Proust describes
Vinteuil's little phrase with great care, but we do
Not hear it. Justice prints six notes of a score.
If we play the notes on the piano as my friend did
For me we hear them now as she plays, and again
now if we listen to the audio file, although even
That's a different kind of now. But we don't hear
Vinteuil's notes at all. We read some (abstract?)
Language (French) that seeks to describe them.
Or, more than likely, we read an English translator's
(abstract?) version that attempts to say in English
What is (now) no longer what Proust wrote, but
Something else. Proust and Justice are no longer
With us. Nor are Vinteuil and Bestor, if they ever
Existed now at all. So let us be content with then.

TIME RETANGLED

But who will play the violin?
Certainly not I
              I'm the mixer in this movie
What's the mix?
The Princess de Guermantes is now the
Three-times married Mme Verdurin, surprise.
The Baron all misled beyond
the pale youth the place is just a name
To practice why deprive yourself
Of pleasure just a little of it that's
Enough but should you find the fixer of this grave
Entanglement I'll lead him to the tangent
Giving him a little shove. *Jupien*, you'll say.
I wouldn't say a thing myself not to
Anyone but you everybody in the circle is
Invited if they form a square
Leave a card or leave the premises
Escorted by the premise

What a lot of lies. And yet what lies ahead ahoy
Is mostly left behind. Do you (*gosh! gosh!*) remember me?
I stood on the terrace of La Raspeltiere, longing,
The short of it too wrong to rhyme.

Or where/what Combray? What/where Balbec?
Would you break a premise for the gardener's boy
Or just continue watching
Soak your gouty foot in the champagne
Hoping by that method simultaneously to cure *la grippe*.
A campaign intended to dishonor you forgotten
As a zeppelin appears and everybody scatters
And did you mean to say the delegate or dignitary
Did some good for your condition at the sanitorium?
We'll stop the cab in order
that the driver tell his sorrow to his little horse
Are you any good at sorrow? Is the weeping driver?
Would you say a Russian come to Paris to

Beckon a new try? But which French composer

Do you have in mind? The guessing game
Has answered frankly, Frank; Fauré finding favor
With the crowd that hissed Saint-Saëns
And doubted Debussy.
It just makes you want to save your skin.
But sometimes when we think that everything is lost
Everything is.

You pessimist. You pest. You paid patrician.
Here are little cakes to dip in teas.
Sweet madeleine, you might instead

Of this hard climb inching all the way
Up tentative Mount Tanglement simply
Drop your dingbat

•   It would interrupt
The silence of your guests, one
Of whom would only speak of duchesses
When only chambermaids compelled the other.
Quelle histoire! In the war the former
Volunteered involuntary memory with
One foot on a higher paving stone.
The latter his epiphanies and puns,
While all the rest were shot and
Bombed and gassed. In elegant surroundings
Mirrors caught M. Beautemps, a feather in his hat,
As he emptied out his flute full of *La Peste*
In what should have been the solo violin's
Little phrase by poor Vinteuil. Another glass?
The old console themselves with news that
Mostly it's the young succumb,
And all the honors go to pesty *pestiferes*.
(Who wants the Goncourt prize in any case,
Said Gide. Young girls in shadow & in flower.

But no rollout of vaccine or booster shot
Will save this demographic. They're given
A placebo for their thoughts at all the endings

Gratis Madame Verdurin, Cottard there
Among them with pastilles. Powder makes
A flash to clarify an image, smooth the wrinkles
On an ancient cheek. The man behind
The camera seems well pleased and bows
And says, *encore, s'il vous plait*. Another line
Of powder, this time up the nose as some-
One takes a break from reading this long book.
Powder also the propellent power slinging
Shells amazing distances—you'd never guess
That sometimes Karl de Bülow wore a little dress.

In the sky the aviator's just reconnaissance.

Many mouths are dry now many hands
Reach out for the pastilles offered happily
By old Cottard. But his practice is
Not efficacious for the guests. The man in
The feathered hat has timed it out,
Has come and gone, *mon cher*. What he left
Behind was Spanish Influenza, I the mixer,
You the mix, got us in this little fix.
Night clings, gives way. Morning brings
The empty streets, the pavements
Of the proud Purveyor
Cool to the feet of those who tiptoe barefoot home.

Instead of an Epilogue

HOMAGE TO SAPPHO

[   ]
[   ]
               ] as if [

       Had written on your behalf [
         ] artfully attired, *poikilóthronos* [

             ] and [
                ] or not [

       Mr. Pound in the metro [
         ] papyrus [

   Platypus in *spring . . . too long . . . Gongula* [